Strangers In
Our Midst

Strangers In Our Midst

PROBLEMS OF THE HOMOSEXUAL IN AMERICAN SOCIETY

By Alfred A. Gross

Executive Secretary
The George W. Henry Foundation

FOREWORD BY C. KILMER MYERS

Public Affairs Press, Washington, D.C.

TO GEORGE W. HENRY
Scholar, Healer, Humanitarian

FOREWORD

Apart from the fact that I was asked to do so, there are three reasons for my writing the Foreword to this book. It was at my suggestion, in the first place, that it came to be written. I had been asked on many occasions if I could recommend a book that would be helpful to ministers who might have to counsel homosexuals. So far as I knew, nothing of the sort was available. There are, of course, the psychiatric textbooks. These are the work of clinicians, whose approach is naturally different from that of the clergyman who could be a tower of strength in an emergency or when he is able to help a troubled person to see the need for consulting a psychiatrist. There are books that deal with what is called pastoral counselling. These, however, presuppose a wider acquaintance with the field of psychology than is usual for the average parish minister to have. There are, of course, the manuals for confessors. It is doubtful that these would fit the requirements of the evangelical pastor.

The more I thought about the matter the more it seemed to me that the long experience of The George W. Henry Foundation in helping the sexually troubled would make it the ideal place to find the material necessary for the preparation of such a book. Many of the Foundation's officers and directors are clergymen. From the day it opened its doors, the clergy have taken responsibility for the day to day problems it encountered. I suggested to the Executive Secretary of the Foundation that perhaps he was in a position to write such a book. What I had in mind was an expository work that would be useful to the minister whose duties only occasionally required him to deal with problems of sexual deviation.

As sometimes happens, the book turned out to be something that neither of us anticipated. The more he became involved in his task, the more the author was persuaded that what he could best do would be to produce an introduction to the problem as a whole, written in terms that would give no difficulty to the veriest layman. He became increasingly convinced that his greatest service would be to offer to the general public a simply written but scholarly book that would serve the needs of those who were desirous of becoming better acquainted with the problem of homosexuality but who lacked the time, the opportunity, or the need to become experts in this area of human behavior.

In the second place, because I am president of The George W. Henry Foundation, it follows that I should have considerable interest in what its Executive Secretary has to say about its years of helpfulness. Although the Foundation is not apt to exercise censorship over the writings of those affiliated with it, and certainly would not require a manuscript from anyone connected with it to be submitted for its *imprimatur*, it is difficult to see how such a work as this would fail to interest those who have oversight of its affairs. Certainly this is not an official pronouncement of the Foundation; the author speaks for himself alone. None the less, what he has to say reflects the general feeling of all engaged in its work.

Nor do I hesitate for a moment to say that this book presents a point of view consistent with those of many respected and responsible theologians. There are many quotations in the book from the writings of D. S. Bailey and David Roberts (to take the first names that come to mind), to whose authority the author appeals from time to time to lend support to what he has said.

He asks us to consider the need for a professedly Christian social order to understand the plight of those who had hitherto vainly called upon it for help. Homosexuals have been made to feel their position so acutely that it is no exaggeration to say of them what the Bishop of Oklahoma has said of another imperfectly understood group of human beings: "When any free person is treated as less than a person, damage is done." To repair this damage by working for a greater degree of understanding is part of the corporate purposes of The George W. Henry Foundation. This it does in conjunction with its usefulness to individuals in time of trouble by helping them find a job or a place to stay; to secure legal aid for those in urgent need thereof; to refer a man to a clergyman who is ready and willing to help him meet a crisis; to get him to a psychiatrist; to aid him find a more secure place for himself. All these things the Foundation does quietly and unobtrusively.

In the third place, the book illustrates the cooperative action of modern science and the Christian faith in dealing with the problem of sexual maladjustment. The war between religion and science (if ever there was one) has long been over. In the pages that follow, we see how many disciplines—the law, social science, theology, perhaps anthropology, psychology, psychiatry, to take a few examples—work together to light the dark streets that house the sexually deviated.

FOREWORD

Many times has the community sought to solve a problem of deviant social behavior by putting the offender in prison. To do this is society's confession of helplessness. Putting a man in jail is an admission that the social thinking has proven inadequate. A prison term is an expedient. Sometimes it has its uses; more often it sends the man back into the world a little worse than when the law sought to deal with his problem by taking him out of the community for a time. More is required to help damaged souls than to cast them into outer darkness.

Strangers In Our Midst is the work of a practitioner of the art of helping people out of trouble; for almost a generation Mr. Gross has been aiding men to solve their problems of sexual deviation. The reader may see for himself what society and churches have done and left undone with respect to those who, up to yesterday, were regarded by the Anglo-Saxon world as objects of grudging tolerance when it felt kindly disposed, and as depraved criminals when it felt otherwise.

Although the author tells us he has written only an introduction to the problem of homosexuality, he has done more than that. He has provided the pastor in search of a helpful manual with a conservative and down-to-earth statement of what is involved. As a matter of fact, it could be recommended by the minister to those coming to him for counsel as a means of becoming better acquainted with their situation as one that involves their relations with themselves, their families, the community and the church. It could also add to the understanding of the homosexual by judges, probation and parole officers, church and social agencies, the physician who comes across the problem in his practice, teachers and guidance people, and so on.

What is said in this brief volume should acquaint its readers with the possibilities of the way of understanding, rather than the way of judgment, in their consideration of the problem. It suggests the need for social action that is rooted in reason rather than emotion. We are all a little dubious about the efficacy of what has been done in the past. To keep from repeating our mistakes will require the participation of men of good will of all faiths and many professions in a practical program that will involve extended research to reach conclusions that are true, sane and workable.

This is a book that speaks to the condition of those who have been left too long to shift for themselves. Up to now, the homosexual has received little justice and less Christian charity. Society and the churches have a stake in the problem of homosexuality. Many of us belong to churches. All are members of society.

C. KILMER MYERS

The Vicarage
Chapel of the Intercession
New York City

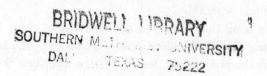

INTRODUCTION

When a witness offers himself as an expert in court, he must establish his right to be heard before he is permitted to give testimony. What is his profession? What academic degrees has he? What books and monographs has he written? With what institution of learning is he affiliated? To what professional societies does he belong? Not until the judge is satisfied that he who offers himself as a witness has demonstrated his qualifications as an expert need any attention be paid to what he has to say. And the courts have been very careful to reserve the right to take or leave the contributions of professional witnesses.

The reader is warned that what follows is not the evidence of an expert. It is the testament of a layman speaking to his lay brethren. It tells something about what he has learned in the course of more than a quarter of a century in the service of The George W. Henry Foundation, which is chartered by the State of New York to help individuals who are unable to come to terms with their problems of sexual maladjustment. Perhaps one might call it a practical consideration of the state of the homosexual in our Anglo-Saxon society. Its point of view is that of a student of social ethics.

Ours is an age of specialization. We are all more or less persuaded that, when we get into trouble, we would do well to send for an expert. This is as it should be. As a matter of fact, the conditions under which we live are such that, if the experts were to cease from functioning, our civilization might fall apart in short order. The experts will be with us for a long time to come, and their number will probably increase and multiply.

Unfortunately a very serious problem arises when we do business with them. Sometimes it is hard for us to follow them. The Cabots among them talk only to the Lowells, and the Lowells talk only to God. To find out what they have to say involves our learning their language. This raises all sorts of difficulties, especially for a layman, who, when he asks a question, is answered in words that are meaningless to him. It may well be that the experts fear that much more harm than good would ensue were they to permit their works to become accessible to the masses. Perhaps they feel a little learning is a dangerous thing.

Dr. Henry once observed that it was possible for a psychiatrist to write a report in English that a high school boy could understand. If the subject of sexual deviations is to be discussed at all, the discussion should be conducted "in a language understanded of the people," avoiding pruriency on the one hand and false modesty on the other. The time has come for society to engage in the serious reconsideration of its assumptions concerning the variations from the accepted modes of sexual activity and interest.

What one thinks of the propriety of permitting the public to share in the examination of this aspect of human nature and conduct depends upon whether the thinker is a Hamiltonian or a Jeffersonian. If it is believed desirable that only the wise, the wealthy and the good should discuss matters of great moment, then there is no need to pursue the subject further. But if one fears with Jefferson what might happen if freedom of expression were restricted to the board of directors of a closed corporation, then a great deal of thought should be given to the dangers inherent in allowing an intellectual *élite* to consider itself the sole custodian of knowledge. Everyone pays lip service to Lord Acton's dictum that power corrupts and absolute power corrupts absolutely. Intellectual power is a dangerous tool to be left uncontrolled in the hands of an oligarchy. Plato to the contrary, an intellectual oligarchy has the same merits and the same defects as any other kind of oligarchy.

Is it necessary for the findings of the scholars to be kept from the generality of mankind? There are, of course, those who feel it better for men to remain in blissful ignorance than to be blown about by every wind of doctrine. When knowledge is hidden away, human curiosity being what it is, sooner or later someone is going to open Pandora's box. And what was kept under lock and key as esoteric and the exclusive possession of its self-appointed guardians spreads downward and outward. The difference between knowledge held in possession by the few and the, watered down version thereof that reaches the many speaks well neither for the disseminators nor what is disseminated.

The trouble with what men think they know about the varieties of sexual experience is that what passes for knowledge is well diluted with half truths, conjectures and downright misinformation. Strenuous efforts are being made to put an end to this lamentable confusion. We hear, for example, reports that homosexuality is on the increase, and that we are rapidly becoming a decadent nation. What do we actually know? Simply this—that the subject of homosexuality is being discussed more freely. There is more talk about the matter than ever before. A very real effort is being made to remove the encrustations of prejudice, fear and suspicion that had made the interchange of ideas regarding the subject difficult, if not impossible. Men of good will are seriously examining the position of the homosexual in our society, and are working to tear down the wall of hostility and misunderstanding that separates those hitherto regarded as members of an alien minority from the rest of society. Many things are breaking up the conspiracy of silence that has thus far prevented full and frank discussion of deviant sexual behavior. We are beginning to see the need to re-examine our fundamental assumptions. What is being accomplished in the behavioral sciences has given men courage to question the validity of the codes regulating sexual activity that hitherto have been regarded as the laws of the Medes and Persians. As never before, men are seeking genuine enlightenment.

During the Second World War, when one thought of going on a motor trip, he was confronted with the necessity of coming to terms with his conscience, as he contemplated the posters demanding to know if the trip were necessary. Is this book necessary? Should it have been written at all? When the torch was about to be applied to the library at Alexandria, someone had the temerity to come to the Caliph and ask him to rescind the order to burn its treasures. The Commander of the Faithful replied that, if the library contained that which agreed with the Koran, it was superfluous and should be put to the flames; if what books were there disagreed with the Koran, they were heretical and therefore worthy of destruction. What does this book accomplish? Can it add a jot or a tittle to what we already know about sexual aberrations? Does it throw new light on what we already know? These and many similar questions suggest themselves to one who dares add to the number of books that profess to enlighten their readers.

Let us see what this book has to offer. Scientific works address themselves to those who are presumed to be able to find their way in them. Many a serious seeker of information comes away empty-handed from books he discovers to be beyond his capacity. Has not the time come for a simpler work to be placed before the general public? Such a book would serve as an introduction to the problem of homosexuality. It would acquaint the intelligent layman with what is being done in the world in which the scholars work. Thus, if he chooses, he is in a better position to find his way in the more erudite studies.

It is quite possible, also, that there is need for a book that will serve as a guide to the individual whose confusion becomes more confounded as he hears the multitude of opinions concerning sex variance. Here, it is hoped, is a book that follows no party line. What is sought in these pages is a *via media*:—between the spokesmen for repression and the advocates of unrestricted sexual activity; between the solid meat of the scholars and the pabulum of the popularizers; between the Scylla of "talking over the head" of the layman and the Charybdis of over-simplification.

There is still another need to be considered. Many ministers seek the means of helpfulness to homosexuals who may bring them their problems. However, they are without desire to become involved in the protracted and highly technical process of psychological counselling. Some have expressed hope for a book to be written that would come to the problem from another point of view than that of the laboratory. Clergymen such as these do not believe themselves lacking in respect for the contributions of the psychiatrists and the psychologists; they feel that the pastor has another and different kind of service to render. They distrust the dogmatism of their brethren who walk after the straitest sect of the Freudians as much as their spiritual progenitors feared the rigidities of the Infallible Church. To them "new presbyter is old priest writ large." The author does not presume to offer his work as a manual for those who are called to the cure of souls. He does feel that it contains material that might be helpful to those who are so engaged.

The problem of homosexuality affects every segment of our society. Even today, it takes courage to discharge our moral obligation to be intelligent about the matter. This becomes understandable when we consider that only yesterday the mentally ill were shamelessly treated, and there are those who still feel that criminals should be punished with severity that stops just short of brutality. When, to take the first example that comes to mind, William Lloyd Garrison dared to speak publicly for the emancipation of Negro slaves, Proper Bostonians looked upon him in much the same way as their present-day descendents might regard a Communist agitator.

Nowadays it is fairly respectable to be interested in the improvement of the condition of the homosexual. The Wolfenden Report in England and the proposals of the American Law Institute for the removal of some of his legal disabilities point to the likelihood of revision of the penal laws in our time. This is as it should be. But much more remains to be done.

Certainly what is done about the unresolved conflicts in the realm of sexual behavior is of concern to all who are interested in bringing about a better social order. To refuse to recognize the seriousness of the matter is futile; to continue in the old ways is to admit defeat. It is time to stop talking about homosexuals and commence to think about people. Homosexuals are people. They are people with a certain set of problems, to be sure; but all sorts of people have all sorts of problems. And the sooner we set about trying to find some workable solutions the better off we will be. Thus far all we have done has been to ostracize, reject and condemn those stigmatized as undesirable. The shortcomings of this method of dealing with a perplexing problem are obvious.

There must be a more excellent way than calling names and pushing human beings out of sight because what they do offends us. And might not the way be found in seeking to understand those whom society has condemned to dwell apart from its common life? If what is said here adds to the understanding of fellow human beings whose sexual behavior bars them from the exercise of full citizenship, then indeed will it help to throw the question of homosexuality open for constructive discussion.

Such merit as this study may have is due to him for whom The George W. Henry Foundation is named. For its manifold defects the author alone is responsible.

ALFRED A. GROSS

The George W. Henry Foundation
New York City

ACKNOWLEDGMENTS

To the publishers, and, in relevant cases, the authors, acknowledgment is gratefully made for permission to use quotations from the works listed below:

Rinehart & Co.: George W. Henry, *All the Sexes*.

Harcourt, Brace & Co.: C. S. Lewis, *Surprised by Joy*; Felix Frankfurter: *Of Laws and Men*; O. W. Holmes: *Collected Legal Papers*.

William Morrow & Co.: Margaret Mead, *Male and Female*.

Weidenfeld & Nicolson: Peter Wildeblood, *A Way of Life*.

Cambridge University Press: Oakeshott, *Social and Political Documents of Contemporary Europe*.

Longmans, Green & Co.: D. S. Bailey, *Homosexuality and the Western Christian Tradition*; A. C. Benson, *Hugh: Memoirs of a Brother*.

W. W. Norton & Co.: Elie A. Cohen, *Human Behavior in a Concentration Camp*.

Yale University Press: Benjamin N. Cardozo, *The Growth of the Law*.

Seabury Press: C. Kilmer Myers, *Light the Dark Streets*.

Oxford University Press: Arnold Toynbee, *An Historian's Approach to Religion*.

Saturday Evening Post: Article by George W. Corner, "*Science and Sex Ethics*."

Simon & Schuster: Essay by Nelson Glueck in *This I Believe*, edited by Edward R. Murrow.

Macmillan Co.: David Bryn Jones, *The Dilemma of the Idealist*.

Dodd, Mead & Co.: Hamilton Wright Mabie, *The Life of the Spirit*.

Noonday Press: Lord Acton, *Lectures on the French Revolution*.

Sheed & Ward: John C. H. Wu, *Fountain of Justice*; Caryll Houselander: *Guilt*.

Harper & Brothers: Raymond B. Fosdick, *Chronicle of a Generation*; E. G. Lee: *Mass Man and Religion*.

Thomas Nelson & Sons: The Holy Bible, *Revised Standard Version*.

Fortune Magazine: Article by Chief Justice Earl Warren, "The Law and the Future."

The first chapter of this book, entitled "The Climate of Opinion," is based on an address delivered before the Mental Hygiene Society of Charlotte, North Carolina, on January 30, 1956. It was subsequently published in the *Psychological Service Center Journal*. The last chapter, the summary and reaching out for a guiding philosophy, is based on two addresses, one delivered before the Divinity School at Yale University, and the other at Trinity College, Hartford, Connecticut. These also appeared, in somewhat different form, in the same journal. Its editor, Dr. Russell G. Leiter, has generously permitted the widest latitude in taking or leaving what had hitherto appeared in print.

The seventh chapter, which treats of the way in which the churches may do some practical things about the problem of homosexuality, is an expansion of an article which was to have appeared in a series commissioned by a church journal that suspended publication. It has been completely rewritten. The same series of articles was to have included the autobiographical fragment, used with its author's permission, that has found its place in the second chapter.

The author would be quite remiss were he not to make mention of his debt of gratitude to those who came or were sent to The George W. Henry Foundation for such service as it could render them. He would like to think that some of them have become his friends. Certainly they have taught him much of what appears in these pages.

Without the encouragement of the President of the Foundation, who set him the task of writing what is said here, the author would have despaired of his ability to complete his work. Father Myers' Foreword tells something of the difficulties that were encountered before the book could be offered for a publisher's consideration. Likewise, gratitude is due to the Vice Presidents of the Foundation, the Reverend Messrs. C. Edward Egan, Jr., and Charles A. Elliott, for reading parts of the manuscript. The inclusion of their names, however, is not to be regarded as signifying their approval of what is said here. Nor does it imply that their respective denominations approve any expression of fact or of opinion. Of the author's debt to Dr. Henry there is no end. Deep, also, is his gratitude to Father William Graham Love, sometime Vice President of the Foundation, who, in his last lingering illness, patiently read and helpfully criticized some of the earlier chapters of the book. The author's deficiencies as a proofreader became increasingly obvious as he floundered in a morass of galleys. The work was generously taken from his shoulders by Mr. Arthur Galligan, long suffering and more-often-than-not unpaid attorney for the Foundation, and a graduate student, Mr. Boris Maysel, who also assumed the labor of compiling the index. Thanks are due to both of these gentlemen for doing what the writer lacked the ability to do. A final word of gratitude is due Mr. M. B. Schnapper, editor of Public Affairs Press, first for his venture of faith in the book, and for his patience with the "moods and tenses" of an author who knows full well that he can try the patience of Job.

Truth seen as the understanding of living people on this earth to-day can make those living people freer, and so better, human beings.

—*Margaret Mead*

CONTENTS

Strangers In
Our Midst

CHAPTER I

THE CLIMATE OF OPINION

"The history of thought is one long record of change; not of restless movement from point to point, but of expansion from stage to stage. In religion there is the same progression, in spite of the passionate efforts of formalists of all creeds to identify the spiritual life with certain unchanging interpretations of facts. The facts remain, but they are seen from different points of view by succeeding generations as the result of that disclosure of life which is always taking place."

—Hamilton Wright Mabie[1]

No man liveth unto himself alone. Robinson Crusoe's Island presented no problems of social organization until Man Friday appeared on the scene. When Man Friday arrived, laws, customs and conventions began to take form. Rules had to be made for the convenient ordering of life. Food had to be obtained; labor had to be performed; and regulations had to be made so that what had become a society could operate smoothly.

Somehow it came to notice that Man Friday had mannerisms of which Robinson Crusoe disapproved. Man Friday picked his nose. Robinson Crusoe had strong notions on the subject of men who picked their noses. He was persuaded that they were not nice people. The more he reflected upon the matter, the more he came to feel that men who behave in this fashion were worse than not quite nice—they were downright immoral.

What could be done on a desert island to put an end to a condition that, unless something were done about it, its ruler felt would drive him mad? For one thing, he could kill Man Friday, and thus be relieved of what had become a source of great unhappiness. He could warn the uncultured boor of the dire fate that awaited him, both in this world and the next, if he persisted in his evil course. He could take a stick and belabor Man Friday mercilessly, both as a punishment for what had now become his sin, and in hope that the beating would reform him. Or he could make Man Friday build a little hut and remain out of sight, thus removing from Crusoe's gaze the spectacle of an untutored savage picking his nose.

This is in essence what all societies must face. They must come to some kind of terms with those in their midst who give annoyance or trouble because their way of life does not conform to that set by

the makers of the standards a community professes to follow. It is not
at all difficult for members of the privileged classes to feel distaste for
the behavior of those less fortunate. The distaste can become disapproval, and the disapproval may express itself in repression, especially when those who fail to conform seem unable or unwilling to mend
their ways. Unconventional manners can easily become bad morals
in the eyes of those who determine what is to be done and what left
undone. And most keepers of morals, both public and private, seem
under the necessity of dealing sternly with the immoral.

There are many ways by which we can persuade ourselves that we
are justified in taking strong measures to curb those whose manners
and morals make us uncomfortable. One way is to assume that
those whose conduct differs from that meeting social approval are
ipso facto evil. This assumption can be entertained without too much
regard for the actualities of the matter. It is easy to believe what we
are told about the bad habits and worse morals of those we have somehow been prepared to dislike. Unflattering stories about them are
accepted as gospel. If repeated often enough, these stories may ultimately find a home in the tribal mythology, and sooner or later
become incorporated into the body of theology.

From time immemorial, the priesthood has had a hand in determining what constituted correct behavior. It helped to decide what
were to be the accepted ways of doing things by each of the gradually
stratifying classes within advancing peoples, as they moved from
nomadic to urban patterns of culture. Forms of civilization, religion
and morality tend to become fixed as societies grow older and more
complex. Organized religion seems fated to align itself on the side of
what St. Paul called the Powers That Be. These, in their turn, make
use of the official ministers and stewards of the religious cults to
discourage those who might threaten their rule.² Needless to say
the possessors of power decided what represented good manners and
good morals. They set themselves up as the aristocracy, and, as such,
reserved all manner of privileges to themselves—including that of dis-
regarding, when it seemed suitable, their own rules. In this they had
the whole-hearted support of their ecclesiastical allies. Both priesthood and aristocracy united to discourage interlopers who might
threaten their control. The others—the "lesser breeds without the
law"—were made to feel their inferiority. They were given concrete
evidence of their lack of status. They became menials, the hewers
of wood and the drawers of water.

Thus were caste and class fixed, and thus in-groups and out-groups

began to take form. Even today primitive totems and taboos are not
without their coercive power. For instance, when a family starts to
sink its roots into a new neighborhood, the parents cautiously feel their
way into what Bagheot called the climate of opinion. They put out
straws to find out what is being done: what the right sort of people
have to eat; how they furnish their homes; where they send their
children to school; what are the better clubs; whether the Democratic
party is respectable in that particular neighborhood; and what is the
right church to attend. Not all of these things can be found in the
pages of Emily Post's convenient handbook of etiquette; there are
many things that have to be learned by trial and error. Some people
learn quickly; for others the learning process is fraught with a great
deal of pain, and there are a few who seem devoid of interest in
finding out how to get along. In effect, every society, great or small,
has an in-group and an out-group. It is apparently the business of
those who constitute the entrenched segment of the community to
make the outsiders feel their lesser estate.

Practically all societies regard conformity as a virtue. Acceptance
of the necessity to conform enables the individual to "know his place"
and cause no difficulty by manifesting outward signs of discontent.
To many the term *nonconformist* contains within itself an element of
contempt. The state demands political conformity, and the churches
esteem theological conformity to be a necessity. Those whose thought
and conduct, when given public expression, differ from the established
ways may be regarded as detrimental to the social or theological order.
When both feel secure, a certain amount of dissent can be tolerated.
But dissenters have to be reminded occasionally of their dubious position, and once in a while it seems necessary for them to be made uncomfortable.

Intolerance need not necessarily be exercised only in matters of great
moment. It can be manifested with respect to matters that do not
commend themselves as being of world-shaking importance. From
Greville's Diaries, for instance, we learn that it was seriously considered that the time had come for Protestant dissenters from the
Established Church to be permitted to take degrees at Oxford and
Cambridge. We are told that the Duke of Wellington was certain that
the world would come to an end if a man were permitted to become a
bachelor of arts without subscribing to the xxxix Articles. This
was in the reign of King William IV, not too much more than a century
and a quarter ago. Yet the world moves. Not only were dissenters

permitted to take degrees; but the time came when, in the next reign, Catholics and Jews were allowed to sit in Parliament.

The opinions and prejudices of those who set the styles of political and religious orthodoxy seep down to the masses. Perhaps they are held somewhat more vividly by those who constitute what used to be called the lower orders. It is not inconceivable that there are those whose drab lives might be made a bit brighter if they feel they share the views of men they consider their betters. This attitude is not unknown in our day and generation. The appeal to snobbery is timeless.

A simple definition of prejudice that is singularly apposite comes to us from the pen of Israel Zangwill. He calls it dislike of the unlike. This has the virtue of accuracy and the merit of understatement. When prejudice is seized upon by skilled manipulators of the masses, the results can be catastrophic for the victims. Tragic is the fate of those selected to bear the brunt of the violence of a mob bent upon wreaking death and destruction. All that is needed is the ability of skilful players upon the crowd's emotions. It can quickly be taught that whatever piety—religious, racial, national— seems to be imperilled demands that those who appear to be its enemies must be ruthlessly wiped out.

Nero played upon the prejudices of the Roman proletariat when he called the early Christians atheists. By making them appear enemies of society, he was able to embark upon a persecution that turned men's minds away from his misgovernment. Thus did Hitler deal with the Jews. Thus the Bolsheviks justified the killing of the remnants of the old Russian aristocracy by calling them enemies of the working class. By so doing, Stalin was able to obtain at least the silence of his countrymen throughout his reign of terror. The nonconformist is always fair game when a scapegoat is needed.

The sexual nonconformist, most notably the homosexual, differs from the others in degree rather than in kind.

Society must live with the long and unpleasant history of its efforts to meet the threat it thought it saw in the homosexual. The social order countered the threat by imposing savage penalties upon men detected in intimacies with other men. Even today, the homosexual is held in general disesteem. He is still the object of harsh penal legislation. He can be the butt of bodily harm at the hands of rough men who need a whipping boy to demonstrate to themselves how manly they are; he can be the recipient of the attentions of those who find it necessary to display their biting comments and crude wit; and he can be held up to contempt by those who ought to know better. By all sorts of unthinking persons who jump to conclusions from evidence that would not convict a petty thief, he has been saddled with a set of unpleasant characteristics that mark only a very small minority of men characterized as homosexual.

The sort of reasoning that in formal logic is called *post hoc ergo propter hoc* makes it possible to see in members of disliked minority groups all sorts of qualities that make their possessors appear unlovely. Nor is it uncommon for those who belong to unpopular minorities to take refuge in ways the majority find objectionable. Unfortunately the objectors fail to take into account their share of responsibility, through their treatment of those whose lives they disapprove, in making the minorities what they are or what the majority think them to be.

Logic has precious little to do with prejudice. Nor has it much more to do with sexual activity or interest. Prejudice and our sexual behavior both have their roots in emotion rather than in intellect. First come the fact and the activity of sex; not until long, long afterward do we come to reflect upon their meaning. Sexual activity is not one that lends itself to cerebration, either in desire or in performance. Even our thoughts in retrospect are highly colored by lights other than those of pure reason.

There has always been a connection in the Anglo-Saxon mind between sex and sin. The Victorian women submitted to what they euphemistically called their husbands' embraces because they felt it incumbent upon them to perform their wifely duties. They considered the sex act a necessary evil. Their views of the logical sequel of the marriage ceremony were colored by a highly emotional distaste.

Sex and smut are words that seem to be connected to each other. It will be a long time before they can be put asunder in the popular mind, dictionary definitions to the contrary notwithstanding. All one has to do is to listen to the franker talk of adolescents; or, for that matter, to what passes for conversation among those presumed to have some acquaintance with the amenities of civilized discourse.

A convention has arisen making the discussion of sexual problems, even of what takes place in the only aspect that meets approval of our western culture as a normal part of the monogamic marriage, something to be avoided, as far as possible, in polite society. Doubtless the learned may talk about the manifestations of sexual behavior in their official bodies; but even these discussions are somehow suspect. If this be true about the activity that is necessary if the human race is to continue, how much more offensive must be talk about the varieties of sexual experience to the host of Mrs. Grundy's relatives. Especially is this true if someone brings up the subject of homosexuality in mixed company.

St. Paul thought it better to marry than to burn. At the most, his approval of the necessary preliminaries to childbirth was grudging. As the notion of asceticism became the ideal of a Christian society, all forms of sexual expression became increasingly illicit in the eyes of the traditional keepers of public morals. Limitations were placed, for instance, even upon the type and frequency of marital relations. There is a state, Georgia, that legislates against what it calls unnatural acts of cohabitation between man and wife. One may assume that the only form of sexual expression that our Western culture approves is in the marriage bed. There are still those whose approval thereof is contingent upon justifying what takes place as necessary for the propagation of the species. To men such as these, sex is not something to be enjoyed, even though the parties thereto were united by a marriage that received the sanction, and even the blessing, of church and state. With this in mind, it is not at all difficult to understand the prejudice that has existed in the public mind against men who found libidinous gratification in ways that lacked this blessing. Especially is this true of those who found gratification with their own sex.

In one way, however, our ancestors were somewhat more fortunate than we are. Seldom in the past was a voice raised to question the authority of society to legislate against forbidden acts. The social and ecclesiastical taboos against sexual irregularity were accepted without question. Ethical relativity was a concept that had no support save in the most remote academic circles. Until yesterday, so to speak, behavior was either right or wrong. Even the contributions of psychiatry to the sexual behavior of men and women were negligible: the psychiatrists were concerned with other matters. Although there was some passing mention of homosexuality in the textbooks, it was not until well into the twentieth century that any great amount of research was undertaken into the causes and conditions of sexual deviations. The studies of the early psychiatrists remained the property of a small group, generally considered more or less esoteric. It is not too many decades ago that the Post Office sought to prevent the importation of Havelock Ellis's books.

After the First World War there was some measure of freedom in discussion of the problems of sexual deviation. Twenty years later in a considerably more liberal atmosphere, Dr. George W. Henry, of the Department of Psychiatry of Cornell University Medical College, was permitted to bring his monumental study of homosexulity before the world.[3] In 1955 this study was followed with what one reviewer called the definitive work on the varieties of sexual experience.[4]

Publication in 1948 of *Sexual Behavior in the Human Male*[5] by Dr. Alfred C. Kinsey, noted University of Indiana biologist, documented what had long been suspected: that the incidence of departures from what were regarded as norms for sexual behavior is much more widespread than had been commonly supposed. A storm burst upon the publication of this Kinsey report. Volume after volume followed, attacking or defending or explaining what the Kinsey investigators had brought to light. The flood of discussion overwhelmed the country; and its repercussions were felt in England and on the Continent. The discussion of the sex variant in our society had at last acquired a certain amount of respectability. We are commencing to see glimmerings of a new climate of opinion with respect to at least the public discussion of sexual activity and interest.

Today the citizen has access to a multitude of works that deal with man's ways of obtaining sexual satisfaction. Most impressive are the scholarly works, chiefly psychiatric in their approach. Then there are the contributions of the popularizers. These are of varying degrees of merit. Some are excellent; others are of questionable value. Too many are ephemeral tracts written in the hope of turning an honest penny to account for their authors. Next come the magazines, some of them condensations of what appears in the learned journals. One or two seem to be not without the ability to titillate. Still others are propagandistic and tendentious. These, too, are of considerable variety.

Homosexuals seem to provide a market for magazines containing photographs of men in scanty attire. Some of these serve the need of those who have difficulty in deciding what is pornography and what is art. Because of the dubious position of the homosexual, it is to be expected that he will be offered a certain amount of literature, so-called, that is not too far from the borderline between the frankly offensive and the more restrained manifestations of the cult of body building. A healthy fear of the wrath of the censors keeps the purveyors of smut in something approximating order. At least downright indecency is not available to the young and easily influenced on the newsstands. Censorship is probably not the ideal way to deal with those who have an eye to the cash value of human susceptibility.

From a hasty examination of several of the publications sold to adolescents and those who should be old enough to give them a wide berth, it is not at all difficult to see how believers in censorship can make a fairly good case for themselves. Like the poor, there will always be with us those who choose to regard liberty as license.

Another manifestation of the changing climate of opinion is to be found in the novels that undertake to depict the folkways of homosexuals. These, too, are of varying degrees of merit. It is doubtful that many of them will stand the test of time. Some of their readers will be individuals who seek to identify themselves with one or another of the characters portrayed in the books. Like the novels that profess to exhibit life in the underworld of the gangster, the "homosexual" novel must have a protagonist who comes to a bad end. The way of transgressor must be made hard.

Finally, there must be considered the homosexual apologetic—the literary justification of his way of life. In this connection, such a work as Andre Gide's *Corydon* immediately comes to mind. An Englishman and an American, both writing pseudonymously, have brought out studies of life in the homosexual community. The American wrote "from a subjective point of view." These have substantial value for the student as expressions of opinion on the part of literate individuals about the world in which they live. To these, in addition to a number of books dealing incidentally with homosexuality in prisons, should be added the works of two British professional writers who served sentences in London penal institutions for homosexual offenses. What they have written about the effects of their experiences makes an important contribution to the understanding of the position of the English sexual deviant.

Periodicals have lately come from the West Coast dealing with a wide range of topics of interest to homosexuals. These are militant in tone, and seek to bring the public to a greater degree of awareness of what must be faced by homosexuals in our society.

A popular view of the homosexual is that of an individual continually in search of companionship, and whose sole preoccupation is the contemplation of the possibilities of physical intimacies. There may be men who fit into this pattern. To the majority, the emotional factors involved go far beyond the achievement of animal satisfaction. The study of homosexual behavior involves much more than the tabulation of orgasms. There are students who feel that the homosexual's great need is for affection, and that he will accept the mechanics of the sex act as a substitute, or a symbol, for what he really desires. This is evidenced by those who speak with the authority of experience of the loneliness of men who must perforce accept the society they can get, rather than the warm associations they seek. These men tell of their quest for the ideal companion with whom they hope to make a superlatively good life. And in that quest many persist, notwithstanding disappointment after disappointment.

The public has been conditioned to see the homosexual only in a certain way. It sees what it has been taught to see—that and nothing more. Since he is not as other men are, it is assumed that the homosexual must be in some way evil. This, in general, is the attitude of the unthinking person. It represents the climate of opinion in the Anglo-Saxon world with which the homosexual must perforce live and move.

It is in similar climates that minorities other than the homosexual make places for themselves. Sometimes it is possible to speak of the contribution of a known homosexual to human enlightenment and progress. This is brushed aside by the prejudiced as the exception that proves the rule. The thinking here is not unlike that of the man who is sure that Jews and Negroes are a bad lot. When the achievements of an eminent Jew or an outstanding Negro are pointed out to such an one, they are dismissed in an offhand manner with a flippant comment that naturally there must be a few good Jews and Negroes. If pressed hard enough, doubtless such persons might be able to hit upon a meritorious homosexual.

Never dare we lose sight of the climate of opinion as a factor in the making of homosexuals. What the world thinks of him is something every homosexual must take into account. He has been taught to regard participation in a certain mode of sexual expression as sinful. Some men refrain from overt activity; but they desire to be punished, and to punish others, for their lusts, as those with a certain type of religious tendencies would put it. There are many more men of this bent than are commonly supposed. They can turn out to be persecutors of their less inhibited brethren. Their attitude toward those who follow their inclinations is that of the dog in the manger.

Another way of discovering the climate of opinion is to be found in psychological tests. Often the person being tested is required to complete sentences in which may be found words with strong emotional overtones. What happens when one is asked to set down words to follow the declaration that: "A homosexual is ..."? It would be interesting to see the responses of a thousand persons, chosen at random. How many write down what they really think? How many find it expedient to say what they thought to be the correct thing?

Today we are not so ready to accept oversimplifications in the realm of sex. The Scriptures tell us of men and women that: "Male and female created He them." [*] But this is susceptible of another reading than the traditional one. Nowadays we are told that all men and women have a certain number of male and female cells. In the well-adjusted male, the male cells predominate. Likewise, in the well-adjusted female, the female cells predominate. But this is an over-simplification. We cannot lay all the blame for the sexual deviations on hormone imbalance. The causes of homosexuality, like those of any sort of diversity within the species, are many and varied. Thus far, no substantial agreement exists among the scientists as to its etiology. Here, however, our primary concern is with the social aspects of the problem.

No matter what the cause, the presence of the homosexual in such great numbers in the body social must concern us. "It is a condition and not a theory," said Grover Cleveland, "that confronts us." When a community becomes alarmed and strikes out against what it preferred to ignore or dismiss with a smile or a sigh, then it is well for society to look deeply into that which causes it concern. When, for instance, a shocking sexual assault is perpetrated upon a child by a senile sex offender, or a particularly vicious rape takes place, a whole community can become panic stricken. In its panic, it will do many things it will later regret—much as Salem repented what it did when it sought to counteract the malign effects of what it considered the prevalence of witches and wizards. A purge of homosexuals is easy to set afoot when someone finds it needful to furnish the public with a convenient scapegoat. Such purges are not unknown in this country or in England. Many brought to ruin hundreds of useful lives and suppressed myriad contributions to the common good. When panic subsides, the community may hang its head in shame, much as some of the inhabitants of Salem lived to regret their witch hunt. Yet there are those hardy souls who would say of homosexuals what the Biblical writer said of witches: thou shalt not suffer a witch to live.

Regardless of perceptible changes in the upper reaches of opinion, the community as a whole cannot be said to look upon the homosexual with friendly eyes. A highly articulate homosexual physician described the popular view as a mixture of shame, fear, horror and fright. These produce hostilities that never sink too far below the surface. All that is needed is for a homosexual to commit a particularly un-

savory offense to revive all the buried dislike of the unlike that goes
to make up the prejudice against him.

It seems inevitable, in attempting to set forth the climate of
opinion in respect to the homosexual, that we will encounter many
differing points of view. The views will vary from unyielding condemnation to enthusiastic endorsement of a sexually deviant way of
life. In the debate in the House of Lords on the Wolfenden Report,
one peer called homosexuals practitioners of unspeakable vice. On
the other hand, there are those who regard homosexuals as chosen
vessels. An admirably brief summary of how the English think is
to be found in C. S. Lewis' autobiography:

" . . . There is much hypocrisy on this theme. People commonly
talk as if every other evil were more tolerable than this. But why?
Because those of us who do not share this vice feel for it a certain
nausea, as we do, say, for necrophilia? I think that of very little rele-
vance to moral judgment. Because it produces permanent perversion? But there is very little evidence that it does . . . Is it then on
Christian grounds? And what Christian, in a society as worldly and
cruel as that of Wyvern [the English 'public' school attended by Mr.
Lewis] would pick out the carnal sins for special reprobation? Cruelty
is surely much more evil than lust and the world is at least as dangerous
as the flesh. The real reason for all the pother is, in my opinion,
neither Christian nor ethical. We attack this vice not because it is
the worst but because it is, by adult standards, the most disreputable
and unmentionable, and happens also to be a crime in English
law. The world will lead you only to hell; but sodomy will lead you
to jail and create a scandal, and lose you your job. The world, to
do it justice, seldom does that." '

Such a view considers homosexuality to be an unpleasant reality
with which English society deals most unrealistically. Despite his own
distaste for what is involved, Mr. Lewis suggests that the efforts of
those who blink it by heated denunciations make precious little sense.
His view is not dissimilar to that expressed by some modern British
writers, perhaps most notably Peter Wildeblood, who had been imprisoned because he was convicted of participating in a homosexual
episode. Mr. Wildeblood speaks of a segment of upper-class British
society in which one can be accepted socially and conduct as many
liaisons with men as seems expedient, so long as his private life is not
unpleasantly brought to public notice. Those who set the standards
of that particular social *milieu* have promulgated a somewhat cynical
Eleventh Commandment: Thou shalt not be found out. Likewise,

much, much lower in the social scale, where nothing seems to matter, one can be as homosexual as circumstances allow, so long as the manifestations thereof do not interest the police. Mr. Lewis suggests what Mr. Wildeblood points out. Quite apart from the morality of the matter, homosexual offenses are committed against middle-class notions of propriety. Homosexuals sin against enthroned respectability. And respectability, when outraged, can become quite violent.

It has been said, probably with a great deal of justification, that the very rich and the very poor can do much as they please in the moral realm. But that statement is subject to considerable qualification. The rich may buy their way out of unpleasant situations; but occasionally a rich or prominent person becomes involved in a scandal which his possessions or importance make it impossible for his lawyers to hush.

The poor still constitute the reservoir that collects the denizens of our prisons. The services of skilled advocates are not at their command to help them escape the consequences of their infringements of the law. None the less, both the very rich and the very poor are allowed a great deal more latitude for their peccadilloes, especially the sexual ones, than their middle-class brethren. Both are equally oblivious of the need to pay much attention to middle-class respectability.

By and large, it is the middle-class individual who is most apt to find his way into the toils of the law. In all probability, the rich man's money will cover a multitude of sins, and the poverty-stricken homosexual is only of casual interest to the public prosecutor. When it comes to blackmail, a wealthy man with a bit of determination can afford to be firm with an extortionist, whose stock in trade vanishes when he discovers that his threats and menaces are meaningless. By the same token, the abjectly poor man need not fear the blackmailer—he has nothing with which to tempt him.

Thus it will be seen that there are many factors involved in our exploration of the climate of opinion in which homosexuals are held. Most of them appear to be emotional. This is seen as we review the furor that followed a United States Senator's charges that a respected Government establishment was a haven for homosexuals. It has become difficult to view the homosexual objectively; too much emotion is involved on the part both of his defenders and denigrators. This is well shown in a recent novel[8] professing to depict life in official Washington, in which a public man takes his life because he faced exposure of an episode that took place many years before. What he feared the people would think, and what the effect of what he had done would be upon his family, not to mention his career, made him feel his situation to be hopeless. This is a part of the world with which every homosexual must reckon.

What can be done? We know enough about the natural history of the homosexual to say that he is not to be held fully responsible for his situation. Surely it is not altogether one of his own devising. Yet what he does will, if found out, in C. S. Lewis' pungent phrase, lead him to jail, create a scandal and cost him his job. And, as Mr. Lewis⁹ sadly concludes, "the world, to do it justice, seldom does that." Nowadays society sends men to prison only as a last resort. By so doing, it admits that it is defeated by a man's crime. When the courts are called upon to deal with an offense viewed less emotionally, they take advantage of the newer penological methods, such as probation, before resorting to the imposition of a prison term.

Judges reflect the state of public opinion when they sit to sentence offenders charged with sexual crimes. How can a judge forget that he must inflict the punishment the law prescribes for participation in an act an English statute called unfit to be mentioned among Christians? Although some legal reform is in sight, and we see a few signs of a new view of the homosexual and his problems on the horizon, we are only beginning to dissipate the effects of centuries-old prejudice and misunderstanding.

More and more information is required to replace unscientific notions of what is involved. Lest we become too impatient, it is important that we bear in mind how society and the churches came to regard homosexuality as a debasement of the sexual instinct and dealt with it accordingly. Dr. Sherwin Bailey, a modern Anglican theologian, who can be considered one of the foremost ecclesiastical authorities on the problem, has traced out for us the development of the church's view of the sexual offender and the homosexual offenses from the story of the destruction of Sodom to the present time. In his definitive work, he says:

"It is clearly of the utmost importance that those who are charged with the administration of the law, those who are being pressed to make changes therein, and all who are concerned with the well-being of society and the maintenance of moral standards, should understand how the Western attitude to homosexual practices originated and developed. If it could be shown that this attitude is based on pre-suppositions, some of which are now untenable, the case in favour of legal reform would be strengthened, and public opinion might become more sympathetic and enlightened."¹⁰

It is obvious that all who concern themselves with the problem of homosexuality are under the necessity of informing themselves how the generally held notions regarding the sexual deviant and his ways and works came into being and how they developed through the ages. Certainly we need accurate information in order to examine critically the assumption that the matter can be disposed of by the repression of those involved and calling it a day. Between such a view and the actualities of the matter there is a great gulf fixed. How to bridge the gulf? It is necessary for us to be wary, lest we confuse emotion and an unsupported tradition with sound judgment. How many of us have given serious thought to what lies behind society's punitive attitude toward those whose sexual problems are still considered unmentionable in many places? How much have we troubled ourselves to examine into the origins and development of the prejudices that find expression in the harsh penalties employed to repress that which is imperfectly understood? It is far easier to go along with accepted opinion than to make the effort to find out the basis for its correctness. The easy approach is to accept the ready-made notion that homosexuals are undesirable, and involvement in their problems must be avoided at all costs. But is the modern social conscience satisfied with that?

A start has been made as a new view is beginning to permeate American society with respect to racial and ethnic minorities. Legislation designed to relieve these groups of some of the handicaps due to discrimination against them stands a chance of ultimate acceptance by the whole people as an aroused social conscience slowly becomes operative. This will take time. Likewise there is talk, and more than talk, of relieving homosexuals of the legal disabilities with which they must live. Expressions of approval by respected men and women of the proposal to remove the homosexual intercourse of two consenting adults from the list of punishable offenses show that there is a chance of modifying our present punitive attitudes. When enough people feel the need for statutory revision, the legislatures will change the laws. In a democratic society, the law is reasonably apt to follow public opinion. And this has its advantages and its disadvantages.

However, legal reform does not tell the whole story. All a more liberal law can do is to point the way for a more enlightened view to find a lodgment for itself in the minds of men. The courts have decreed that Negro children must be integrated into the public school system. Still this does not make their position an altogether happy one. It is hard enough to legislate tolerance into a people. How much more difficult is it to secure the acceptance of an unpopular brother! None the less, the removal of the legal disabilities under which a minority labors is a step toward its emancipation and ultimate acceptance.

Much more can be done to alleviate the condition of the homosexual strangers and sojourners among us if a sufficient number of men of good will are impelled to make this their concern. To do this requires more than lip service to our common faith that every member of a free society is entitled to the opportunity to find his rightful place and assume his full share of responsibility.

By no stretch of the imagination may the world in which the homosexual is obliged to dwell be called the best of all possible worlds. But it can be made better. How this is to be brought about is another matter.

CHAPTER II

WHAT IS A HOMOSEXUAL?

For now we see through a glass darkly.
—I Cor. xiii:12

We have begun our exploration of the world with which the homosexual must come to terms by gaining some acquaintance with the climate of opinion in which he lives. We have been using the term *homosexual* as though everyone knew what was involved therein. Is this a safe assumption? Let us see if we can frame a definition that is capable of fairly general acceptance. How go about this? For one thing, we might begin by seeing how the stories of three men whom the courts found guilty of homosexual offenses throw light on what is involved. What common factors appear in all three stories? And can we, from these factors, discover what a homosexual is?

First let us look at Tom. As was his custom, he and some friends from the office where he was regarded as a rising young executive, stopped at a college club to end the day's business with a drink. When the time came for the group to break up, Tom was feeling a bit mellow. He insisted that he was not intoxicated. Here is a man of about thirty, who had been married for seven years, and the father of a boy almost five years old. He had a very correct home in a very correct Westchester suburb. His well-to-do parents had sent him to the "right" preparatory school and the "right" college. He managed to get himself elected to one of the "right" fraternities. So far as outward appearances were concerned, Tom was a substantial citizen, well on his way to a substantial career. Most decidedly he was a conformist. All in all, Tom would appear to be typical of upper middle class America. He served creditably on the board of governors of a country club; he did just as well on the school board in his town; and of course he served his country with some distinction in the Korean War. He had every reason to look to the future with confidence. Or so it would appear.

Because he had quite a bit of drink in him, Tom found it necessary to stop in the washroom at the railroad station on his way home. While there, a stranger approached him and made sexual advances. Tom permitted these to continue to the place where a detective thought he had observed enough to arrest both Tom and the stranger. They were charged with the commission of homosexual disorderly conduct. When questioned some days later, Tom readily admitted intimacies with men—although never twice with the same person. He said these episodes were meaningless to him and were speedily forgotten. He doubted if he would be able to recognize any of the casual acquaintances with whom he had engaged in sex play.

Tom insisted that he loved his wife and child, and felt that his home life was happy. So far as he was concerned, the occasional homosexual adventure into which he drifted meant no more or no less than the occasional adultery that took place and was condoned in the social set in which he moved.

When he appeared before the court, the judge, on the basis of Tom's previous good record, decided to suspend sentence. Tom was warned that if he were rearrested for a similar offense, he would find himself in a most unpleasant situation. He was given to understand that society took a very dim view of that type of public behavior. The criminal charge could have meant ruin for Tom. Yet to him the whole sordid business was something quite insignificant and meaningless, save for the annoyance caused him by the trouble to which the law had put him. Is Tom a homosexual?

Dick is vaguely effeminate. Perhaps a better word for him would be ineffective. There is nothing outstanding about him: he is a mousy little man. Save to those with a weather eye for such matters, it is doubtful that anyone would have paid much attention to Dick's sex life. A worldly wise lawyer thought his troubles might stem from it being a matter of some question whether anyone paid attention to him at all. He plodded through a drab existence.

Dick made his home with an ailing mother who "enjoyed poor health." The mother professed the hope that her son would marry; but she saw to it that no girl he brought home for the maternal inspection could be considered suitable. He made love quite chastely to a succession of school teachers, librarians and other workers in genteel occupations. One social worker shocked him by her verbal assaults upon his prudishness. In no case did he pursue his amorous adventures with women (and there were not many of them) beyond a tepid kiss.

Such feeble sexual satisfaction as Dick was able to obtain he got from chance met male acquaintances. What took place between them was at best hole-and-corner intimacies. Dick met his Nemesis in Central Park. An able-bodied male engaged him in conversation, and led him on to the point where he felt safe enough to do that which caused his new-found friend to make proclamation that he was a detective and place him under arrest. Now Dick has a court record of conviction for homosexual disorderly conduct. Is Dick a homosexual?

In the language of Times Square area of New York, Harry is a "hustler". Thus far he has been able to keep himself from being accused of really serious crime. He is twenty years old. Already he has a long record of petty offenses; but the longest time he has been required to stay in prison has been a thirty day sentence for participating in a drunken brawl.

Harry loiters around a district where homosexuals are known to come in search of young men with whom they can be intimate for a price. He indignantly denies that he is a "fag", a "homo", or a "queer". Yet he readily permits those with the desire and the means to have homosexual relations with him, so long as the customer is willing to play what is called the female role in the transaction. Harry feels himself to be preserving his masculinity by being the "man" in acts of homosexual intercourse. Or so he says. He finds it necessary loudly and vehemently to call attention to his masculinity; and he tells anyone who will listen to him that he derives absolutely no pleasure from what he does for money. He vociferously brags about his adequacy with females, and asserts that much of what he gets as payment for his services to men is spent upon his women. The uncharitable would call Harry a male prostitute.

From early childhood, he had been a source of trouble to the authorities in the small town from which he fled to New York. On his own admission, he is a liar and a thief. He quit school as soon as the law permitted. At home he might hold an ill-paying job for a very short time; but he always managed to find himself without work. Finally the sheriff's men ordered him to leave town. He found his way to New York and made some feeble efforts to find work. He went hungry for a few days until he discovered the possibilities of Times Square. There he met a man who bought him a meal, arranged for a night's lodging, and had sex with him. Thus began Harry's career as a "hustler."

He rapidly learned from his fellow "hustlers" how to get along in the prostitute's half world. He quickly learned all the tricks of the trade, and became acquainted with its financial possibilities. Of course he placed a high value on his capacities to entertain his patrons; but there were few offers that went unheeded because the price offered did not meet his expectations. Occasionally, when a client attempted to repudiate his bargain, Harry would resort to violence. For the most part, he is a lazy soul, and will brawl only on considerable provocation. He is more apt to take what the gods provide. He may find it necessary to boast to his fellows about the beatings he inflicts on refractory customers; but the beatings were more likely to be the product of Harry's imagination; they were recounted to impress the fellow members of his craft with his male prowess. A probation officer who investigated him in the course of one of his frequent court appearances called his a disorderly, aimless existence. Is Harry a homosexual?

What is a homosexual? The *Oxford Dictionary* defines him as one "having a sexual propensity for persons of his own sex." This is an admirable description of an important part of the homosexual's way of life. It tells how he derives what the psychiatrists call his libidinous gratification. But does it define him? Does it tell what he is? Certainly it provides us with a starting point. We are given a common factor by which to distinguish him from those whose sexual propensities run in other channels. Is that enough?

The dictionary comes to its definition by employing the method of Aristotle. When he saw a sufficient number of objects resembling one another closely enough that all had certain properties in common, he put them in a category and gave the category a name. He arrived (let us say) at the notion of a chair by observing a number of things with enough common characteristics that any one of them could be fitted into a category. This category received the name *chair*. In varying degrees, all had the property that could be described as *chairness*—to coin a clumsy word. Therefore all objects having the attributes of *chairness* could be called chairs; and everyone knew what was being talked about. Even though chair might differ from chair in many aspects, there were enough elements all had in common that a chair could be recognized by the observer as such. The dictionary definition of the word *homosexual* is based on the fact that a very large number of men have been observed to have a sexual propensity for their own sex. It was possible, therefore, to describe men having these propensities as homosexual. And, as there are chairs and chairs, there are homosexuals and homosexuals.

Enough similarity of sexual behavior appears in the cases of known homosexuals for the term to have a great deal of meaning. Sufficient common phenomena are present for us to say that the homosexual has a special way of deriving his sexual satisfactions; and that differs from the more conventional ways of so doing. It is on the basis of this distinction that the dictionary defines the homosexual.

But it is doubtful that how the homosexual seeks and finds sexual satisfaction tells the whole story of those so characterized.

Some homosexuals are well-educated individuals; others are illiterate. Some occupy positions of great power and influence; others are barely able to hold a job that makes no particular demands on its holder. Some struggle to remain in communion with one or another of the churches; others have deserted religion. Some have great possessions; others barely manage to exist. Some are good citizens in all respects save for their sexual behavior that is against the law; others are confirmed criminals. Some distinguished themselves in the armed forces of their country; others seized upon the opportunity to gain deferment from service on grounds of unfitness. And so it goes. It requires but the most cursory glance to see that there are all sorts and conditions of homosexuals.

This can be seen as we look into the histories of the men of whose stories brief fragments appear at the beginning of this chapter: all three of whom came to the notice of The George W. Henry Foundation as homosexual. In varying degrees, all three had a sexual propensity for their own sex. All three seemed to derive satisfaction from the physical exercise of that propensity. Are all of them homosexual? There is no doubt that all had had relations with men. The quality and quantity of the relations differed from individual to individual. Tom, the rising young man of affairs, reports occasional intimacies with men whose acquaintances were speedily made, and, after they had served their purpose, their existence speedily forgotten. He states that he is also sexually adequate with women, and has a wife and child to show for it. He is probably what is called a bi-sexual. Such physical intimacies as fell to the lot of Dick, the school teacher, were with men. He admits that that is where his interests lie. To gratify the conventions, he put out an occasional feeler in the direction of women whom he was sure would make no real demands upon him. When one tried to push him further than he was willing to go, he fled precipitately. If by his fruits he shall be known, Dick is a homosexual. There is a chance, however, that, because of his need for conformity, his vague strivings after women might be made into something more concrete. As to Harry, the "hustler", he could probably be called a bi-sexual, depending upon how much credence one places in his stories. It is certain, however, that he makes his living from what he gets for his sexual services to men.[1]

The use of the term *homosexual* is apt to prove misleading. Certainly it is used to cover a multitude of variant sexual experiences.

Yet in every one regarded as so conditioned, there is some degree of attraction to his own sex. Thus the Kinsey Report carefully tabulated the sexual experiences of the men who gave information about their behavior to the investigators. It was learned from those who responded to the questionnaires that they engaged in all types and gradations of sexual experiences, ranging from exclusive performance with men to exclusive performance with women, with a great variety of shadings in between. The accuracy of the reports need not be considered here. What is important, from the standpoint of the social study of the problem, is that the departures from the accepted norms of sexual behavior are much more widespread than had hitherto been believed. They affect every stratum of society, from the economically secure to the denizens of Skid Row. Nor, so far as can be determined, were there any ethnic or religious groups whose members did not report homosexual experimentation. It is evident that the problem affects the whole body social. No social segment, racial or religious group is exempt.

The popular notion of the homosexual has very little to commend it in the way of accuracy. The contemptuous epithet fairy, which serves to characterize what is almost certainly a minority of those engaged in overt homosexual relations, is the stereotype by which the unthinking picture all whose behavior departs from the conventional in respect to sexual activity. The fairy seems under some compulsion to make himself conspicuous by speech, dress, and deportment in order to invite attention to his idiosyncrasies. For every one so recognizable, there must be a hundred homosexuals sufficiently inconspicuous to go their way unnoticed; save, perhaps, by the few who have an eye to such matters. Thus, as we attempt to draw up a definition of the homosexual, we must constantly bear in mind that what is on public view tells only a small part of the story. For the most part, we deal with those who, save in the instance of the exhibitionists among them, are but little indistinguishable from other men.

In another place*, it was suggested that the homosexual might be in the uncomfortable position of the occasional Jew or the occasional Negro who sought to "pass" as something else. There is a fairly considerable literature on the subject of "passing", and what it does to the personalities of those who try to live as something they are not. In this connection, it might be helpful to consider the case of a very light Negro, almost indistinguishable from a white person, who ventures into a place where Negroes are the subject of vilification. What does this do to the personality of him who must perforce listen to what

is being said? Does he feel he must outdo the others in drawing
attention away from himself? What happens when an inconspicuous
homosexual finds his way into a group expressing itself vulgarly about
those who must be mentioned only with scorn for the speaker to be
able to prove that he has all the attributes of masculinity? What sort
of masculinity is it that needs to demonstrate its adequacy by deni-
grating "queers," "fags", or "homos"?

Minority groups find themselves condemned because their members
try to make places in the sun for themselves. When, for instance,
Jews or Negroes try to become integrated into the population, they
are called pushing and aggressive. If they stay within the confines
of their groups, keeping themselves to themselves, as the old phrase
has it, then they are considered unassimilated. Such is the "damned-
if-they-do" and "damned-if-they-don't" attitude that meets those
whose misfortune it is to be somewhat different. Those who dislike
minorities that stay in their own back yards should occasionally
give some thought to why the streets seem uninviting. Why is it
necessary for members of a minority to withdraw into their protective
shells? And how much responsibility for keeping them there can be
lodged on the majority's doorstep? Homosexuals who consider themselves to belong to a minority make out a fairly good case for themselves.

As we proceed to a formulation of our definition of the homo-sexual,
we can observe that he is distinguishable for certain idiosyncrasies of
sexual behavior. By reason of these idiosyncrasies, he is marked off,
or marks himself off, from those who behave more conventionally.
Just or unjust, accept it or reject it, this is the way the homosexual
is regarded by the world.

Varieties of sexual experience have been observed since the time
when men first began to record how human beings behaved. The
anthropologists have informed us how primitive peoples regarded those
whose ways of finding sexual gratification were out of keeping, with
the ones generally followed. And there are great differences in the
manner in which early primitive societies and today's equally primitive
cultures look upon the sexual deviators within their borders. The
development of the ideas of Western Christendom in respect to the
homosexual is to be found by those to whom this is important in Dr.
Bailey's indispensable work.[3] From it we learn that the disesteem in
which the Church has held him is as old as the institution itself.

Greek society entertained a much different view of the sexual behavior of men; it was even a bit more tolerant with respect to women

who lived outside the yoke of marriage. The acceptance of the homosexual was quite matter of fact. This is made manifest when we recall that the classic literature contained not a few passages in praise of what were considered elevating homosexual relationships. In the Hellenic world, a warmly affectionate relation between two soldiers, probably involving physical intimacies, was neither condemned nor condoned. It was simply part of a tradition. It was assumed, notably in the army of Sparta, the warlike Greek city-state, that instruction by an older man of his younger comrade in the art of war might include a certain amount of warmth and affection that could find sexual expression. Certainly there was a time in Athens when no one seems to have called the morality of homosexual relationships into question. However, Plato is not above a quip, in one of his dialogues, at the expense of Socrates, well on in years, assiduously pursuing young men. The difference between the Greek notion of *laissez-faire* in sexual matters and the rigidity of the Hebrews is illustrated by a classroom remark of a distinguished professor of philosophy who followed the Hebrew view, mediated through the Old Testament and the Puritan tradition. He deplored Plato's acceptance of homosexuality as a defence of what he called "animalic bestiality."

As time went on, Greek legislators did find it necessary to curb sexual freedom that bordered on license. They took steps to limit its excesses, protecting slaves and aliens by law from assaults by citizens. In Imperial Rome, there was little or no pretense of moderation. The Greek notion of measure in all things was lost in a sea of debauchery. Or so, at least, the classic writers tell us.

There is a suggestion of the prevalence of homosexuality in knightly circles in the Middle Ages. Certainly charges of wholesale homosexual indulgence were flung about with a lavish hand when the King of France set up a court to get rid of the Templars. The knight-errant had to find sexual release somewhere, as he rode off to wars with his lady's favor attached to his armor. What went on among the merchants and peasants no chronicler troubled to record. And there persist to this day vestiges of the notion that homosexuality is a vice of the upper classes.

The Reformation put an end to any freedom of sexual expression that may have gone on quietly through the Middle Ages. Social controls were tightened in the interest of the militant puritanism that had come into power. A statute of King Henry viii prescribed the death penalty for those detected in homosexual intercourse that was called "the abominable and detestable crime against nature, not to be

mentioned among Christians." That way of regarding the homosexual
offenses and those engaged therein has been followed, with very little
change, to this day. There has, of course, been considerable human-
ization of the punishment. A description of the homosexual, if couched
in the language applied to him by the penal laws, would make him
appear, as one student put it, just a little bit lower than the untouch-
ables of India.

What is a homosexual? We could continue endlessly in our quest
for a definition that would do something more than describe his behavior. Perhaps it would help if we were to become acquainted with
what one homosexual has to say about himself and his situation. It is
the story of a young man who had to pay the price of imprisonment
that society exacts for disobedience to its statutes. Here is an account
of what happened to an individual who lived in a fair sized town, who
was caught in a vice crusade. He came of good family; he had a fine
job and an excellent work record; he was well-educated; and he enjoyed the respect of his fellow townsmen—until the blow fell. When
he served his term he returned to his native place. Not only did he
find it impossible to obtain work commensurate with his abilities, but
there seemed little chance of his being able to obtain any sort of responsible job. It became increasingly evident that the community
would not let him live down the stigma of imprisonment. He felt he
would have to make his own future elsewhere. An opportunity was
arranged for him to work in a distant city, where he held a responsible
position for over a year. This became a springboard to more lucrative employment in which he was able to put his training to better
advantage. After several years, he seems to be moving toward success
in his chosen profession.

The young man reports that the shock of his arrest and the fact
of his imprisonment put an end to his homosexual experimentation.
Under the guidance of a psychiatrist and a trained clergyman, he
has been able to come to some conclusions respecting the way of life
he proposes to follow. Essentially a conformist and a conservative,
the man's desire for conformity reinforced his felt need to make drastic
changes in his mode of sexual expression. As far as can be determined,
he no longer regards himself as a homosexual. Several years ago, The
George W. Henry Foundation was aproached by the editor of a now
defunct church periodical to arrange for a series of articles on homosexuality that never saw the light of day. A psychiatrist, a clergyman and a sociologist were asked to contribute to the series and
the Foundation was able to deliver something from a homosexual who

was literate enough to produce a meaningful article. What follows comes from the pen of the young man whose story is briefly touched upon here. With his permission, and with the assurance that a few minor changes would be made to prevent any possibility of identification, what he has to say is presented for publication.

I AM A HOMOSEXUAL

By An Anonymous Author

I am a homosexual, a convicted felon. I have served time in a State prison. Now I am on parole, trying to win my way back to the place in society I had forfeited. So far as I can see, I have no hostility toward those who prosecuted me. The district attorney who had to send me to jail told me how much he regretted a painful necessity. This is the story of how one man had to learn what it really means to be a member of a shunned, outcast group. No clergyman or psychiatrist, no matter how sympathetic he may be, can really know what it means to live in constant fear—as every homosexual must and does live.

I am an average sort—not too tall and certainly not short; not fat, perhaps a bit on the lean side. I am youngish—thirty or so. It is doubtful that anyone would look at me twice. I could pass unnoticed on any college campus, or on Park Avenue or Beacon Hill, or their counterparts in Chicago or San Francisco. I could be any middle class young man. My psychiatrist and the clergyman who are trying to help me—both of them knowing their way around in such matters—tell me that, so far as they can see, I bear none of the marks by which the man in the street believes he can recognize the homosexual. I could be anyone in a big city.

I am not alone. There are numberless men like me. And women, too. They come from all walks of life. I speak for the silent—what a reformed communist called the faceless men. Nor can I reveal my identity. Apart from my fear of losing a good job, although my trouble is known to my employer, there are others to be considered,—my family, the few friends who stood by me and trusted me in the town where I had lived all my life. Nor have I, so far as I know, any desire to exploit my experiences. I need anonymity. The minister in my home town who felt that I could write assured me that I could help others through telling what happened to me. He asked me to put aside a natural reluctance to talk about painful things and faithfully promised me protection from prying eyes.

Until I was taken to prison, I lived and worked in a good sized town. My family had been there for generations. I was a member of the professional class——with a certain amount of standing in a community where, a few years ago, there were not too many college graduates. I lived on the right side of the railroad tracks. I had an interesting job and a chance to rise in the word. The future seemed to hold promise for a respected career as a conventional, middle class American.

I considered myself an average sort of Christian. I could not call myself conspicuously devout, although I attended church regularly enough. I was financially honest. The temptation to steal never arose—I was doing well enough financially, and I had about what I wanted. I suppose I told as few lies as the next. I looked upon myself as a young man on the way up.

There was a problem in my life with which I could not cope on any terms. I was a homosexual. How I became one is not for me to say. There was no one to whom

I could bring my problem. I was afraid to talk to my minister—he expressed himself vehemently against what he called degenerates. Although I consider myself of better than average intelligence, I never thought of consulting a psychiatrist. Psychiatrists, where I came from, were for the insane. And I never had any fears for my sanity.

I was not proud of my state. I hated it, and I hated myself. And yet I continued in it. There are those who say that a homosexual must accept himself for what he is. This I could not do. The few contacts I had were with persons and in places that could only be described as sordid. When they were over, I wanted to get away as quickly as possible. Usually I went with male prostitutes, whom I never wanted to see again.

I have never regarded myself as a member of a homosexual community. There were no places in my town where homosexuals could get together. I led two lives—my public life as a rising young man who was becoming an important member of society and a secret, shameful life. This I lived when loneliness, bitterness and frustration drove me out to find—more truthfully to buy—companionship.

A preacher began a campaign against what he called "male vice." The newspapers took it up, and several prominent men were sent to prison. My turn came. I was arrested and sentenced to State Prison. After their fashion, the officials and keepers were kind; I experienced no cruel treatment. The time came for my case to be reviewed by the Parole Board. Before I could be released, it was necessary for me to have a job that would meet the approval of the State officials. It was impossible for me to return to my former job. My employers felt that the community would not tolerate an ex-convict on their staff, especially one who had been involved in a sex scandal. After many vain attempts to find suitable employment, a business man in my community said he would take a chance and give me a job as a clerk. The Parole Board set the day for my discharge from prison.

When I was given my freedom, I returned to my parents' home. My mother and father were simple, unsophisticated, elderly people. To this day I doubt if they fully understood the nature of the charge that required me to be sent to the penitentiary. Maybe it was fortunate for them. They stood by me, loyally and unquestioningly, visiting me reguarly when the rules allowed me to have visitors. They gave me a home when I returned and asked me no questions.

A clergyman and a psychiatrist in my home town were also waiting for me. They began treatment and counselling to help me to understand what had happened. The minister offered me acceptance and did everything within his power to get me to accept myself as a person. It was hard for me to believe that the finger of scorn was not pointed at me twenty-four hours a day. I was sure that, when a couple of friends nodded to me on the street, they would say, as soon as I got out of earshot: "There goes that ex-convict. You know why they sent him to prison."

Soon we began to take stock to see what could be done to put the pieces together. Doctor and minister insisted that I had to stop living in fear of what people might say about me. I had been in prison; I had committed a homosexual offense; these were facts; and all the wishful thinking in the world could not make them a bad dream. So what? I finally was able to believe that there were other jobs in the world than the one I had lost, and that there was still a great deal of work somewhere that I would be able to do. My advisers insisted that it was up to me to make a serious search for it. Another worry haunted me. The job I had was something for which I was thankful. But I had no particular talents as a clerk. My boss was generous enough not to complain about my mistakes; but I was sure he would not be too unhappy if I were to find something else to do.

The clergyman and the psychiatrist had a friend in a great city a thousand miles away. They wrote him and asked if he could do something about finding work for me that would utilize my education and what they were kind enough to call my valuable experience. Weeks went by and there was no answer. I began to lose hope that anything would come of it. One day I received a telephone call from the psychiatrist to come to his office immediately. He had received a letter from his friend stating that the vice president of a large organization wanted to see me. The next thing I knew I was sitting in a luxurious office, talking to an important man who calmly informed me that he had heard all he desired to know about my case. So far as he was concerned, he was ready to put me to work the next day. He then said, "If anything gets out about your troubles, it will be because you talked out of turn." Then he smiled and said, "Let's go and get some lunch and we'll try to find out what you can do to earn your keep with us."

The job that was to be the gateway to my new career began with the next day. Perhaps it was a bit too easy for me, after all. I had not been there for six months, when I began to feel that I had learned all I could about my job. I commenced to think promotion was slow in coming my way. I was sure that I could do something much more responsible than the routine job I held down. Surely I appreciated an unbelievable stroke of good luck; but I was human enough to feel that, once I had demonstrated my ability to do a good job, I should be given to chance to show what I could really do. It was all too easy for me to forget that I had been inside a jail as a prisoner. And I was sure that everybody else ought to forget it. But life isn't quite as simple as all that.

Once in a while I received reminders that society still had some interest in me. My parole supervision had been transferred to my new place of residence. I had to become acquainted with a strict parole officer and learn occasionally that, so far as he was concerned, I was just another prisoner. Maybe that was good for me. Arrangements were made for me to see a new psychiatrist. A minister in the midst of running a back-breaking slum parish found time to write me that his colleague back home had wanted me to see him, if time could be found. He saw me regularly once a week. Thus I took up the threads of treatment.

To-day I ask myself what I had hoped to gain from my life as a homosexual. As I look back, what stands out is my loneliness and how much I needed someone to make life less lonely. I doubt if I really deceived myself into thinking that any of the boys I picked up might develop a real affection for me. But they could help me for a moment or two to forget it, and pretend that I was experiencing some sort of happiness. But, when I looked around town and saw the men who said they found happiness in that way, I felt revolted. I hated them, and I hated myself. It is not for me to say how others should pursue happiness. I do say that theirs is not the life for me.

Now I am on the way back. It is too early to say much about what the future holds for me. There was no chance for me in a community that knew I was an ex-convict. Before I went to prison, I feared to talk about my problem. All I could do was to try to convince myself that I would not have to live with it tomorrow. But that tomorrow never came. My psychiatrist told me, and I believe him, that I was deceiving myself. He said I was so sure that there was no help for me that un-

consciously I was doing everything I could to get myself arrested and get the punishment I was sure was coming to me. It is hard to accept this.

   What happened to me could have happened to anyone with the same sort of problem. I was fortunate to be given help when I needed it, and doubly fortunate
in having the sense to know that it was necessary for me to take what was offered.
There is quite a bit of lost time to be made up. Just how one manages to live
down a prison term and make a respected place in society is not quite clear. Others
have done it. So can I. Certainly there is no more need for self-deception and self
pity. I have still a hard row to hoe; but, with my eyes open, there is a chance that
the new life I make for myself will rest on a solid foundation.[4]

   Is this what the average citizen considers to be the life of a homosexual? Could it not just as easily be the story of any young man, of
middle-class origins and standards, who "made a mistake" and was
paying the price society demands of its erring members? Certainly
it is anything but typical of the homosexual who, in the popular mind,
devotes all his energies to the pursuit of sexual pleasure.

   Save for the way by which he gratified his sexual needs, this young
man was justified in describing himself as an average sort of person.
He seemed like any of the thousands of young men from the provinces
who come to seek their fortunes in New York. Here is an apt illustration of what, twenty years ago, we called an orderly homosexual. Most
of the men so designated, however, had the good fortune to escape a
prison term. Certainly he was correct in saying that his advisers knew
what they were talking about when they told him that in all probability
no one would look at him twice—unless he chose to call attention to
himself.

   By and large, and even including the exaggerated mannerisms of the
exhibitionists, the homosexual differs from other men only in the way
he finds sexual satisfaction. The distinguishing marks of effeminacy
and boisterous behavior that characterize the "fairies" are not present
in the majority of men whose sexual propensities lie in the direction of
their own sex. It becomes increasingly evident that he who would
understand the homosexual must take into account the social disesteem in which he is held. Likewise he must consider the many
varieties of homosexual experience, and the categories it is possible
to set up within the ranks of those whose sexual behavior welds them
together into some sort of community.

   Society has a way of dealing unpleasantly with those who manage
to call attention to their nonconformity. It is not unusual for students
to consider the homosexual in similar case to the men and women who
might belong to any unpopular minority. To some it might appear
an irreverent analogy: but is there not a surface resemblance between

the life of the homosexual in our society and the underground existence
of the early Christians in Rome in the time (let us say) of Nero? The
nascent church consistuted a small community of the faithful who
dwelt as far apart from the corrupting influences of the metropolis
as possible. Of this society within a society, only a few of its members could be found in the more affluent places. The majority—slaves,
peddlers, tradesmen, artisans, uprooted persons, poor aliens, house-
wives—were members of the urban proletariat. Nowadays we might
call them second-class citizens.

Save for his unorthodox way of expressing himself sexually, the
homosexual is paid as much attention in a great metropolitan Anglo-
Saxon community as Rome paid to Androcles, the little Greek tailor
in Shaw's play. Androcles was a fairly useful member of society. He
got into trouble because he adopted an unorthodox way of expressing
himself religiously, thus causing a breach of the peace. Or so its
keepers thought. To the cynical, his might be a nuisance value.[5]

Thus far, our attempt to define the homosexual has contemplated
individuals who were presumed to exercise a certain freedom of choice
in securing suitable sex objects. What about those who drift into
homosexual practices through force of external circumstances? What
about the additional compulsions that need not be taken into account
by those who have some limited freedom of selection? Is not the
case somewhat different when we consider what might happen to any
individual, ordinarily otherwise predisposed, who finds himself without
access to women? It is a commonplace that few will long remain continent under those circumstances. Sooner or later they will employ
less conventional methods of finding sex objects. A certain amount
of homosexual experimentation may be expected when they are deprived of ordinary outlets for a sufficient length of time.

Schools and colleges, prisons, military and naval establishments, and
all places where access to acceptable sexual partners is non-existent
or too difficult, inevitably face this problem. Many youths who have
been graduated into the ranks of the hoodlum homosexuals or male
prostitutes tell of their introduction to homosexual practices in orphan-
ages or "reform" schools. There, of course, inmates are given no encouragement to find their way sexually. Their only outlets are mas-
turbation and experimentation with their own sex. And, when
caught, they may expect severe, even brutal, punishment for their violations of the rules. Because of society's prejudices, sex instruction
of an intelligent sort is the last thing one expects to find in the curriculum of such an institution. All the inmates learn from officialdom is

that any sexual activity is evil and that continence is expected of them until the time comes to marry and carry out the obligation to propagate the race. Such is the official teaching; unofficially they acquire a lurid stock of misinformation about sex from their peers or sadistic or moralistic officials. What is told them seldom corresponds to the facts of the matter.

When a prison inmate's term expires, or a soldier or sailor receives his discharge from the service, what happens to men who have availed themselves of homosexual outlets? When they return to the community, do they seek more conventional sexual opportunities of the sort that proved gratifying when they had access· to them? Or, having found a new mode of sexual expression, do they continue to seek and find male sex objects? An old-time prison official remarked that it sometimes struck him as the supreme irony of the penal system to put homosexuals in jail. Too often the advent of a known homosexual was regarded by his fellow inmates as something of a godsend. All it did was to make available to such a one a horde of sex-starved men. It is doubtful that the best intentioned invigilation and the segregation of known homosexuals can accomplish much more than help the penal administration to say that it does its best to stamp out what could become the occasion of a prison riot.

Apparently the need for homosexual outlets could not be denied, even in so depressing a place as a concentration camp in Hitler's Germany. In an important book discussing the effects of confinement upon the personalities of the victims of a vicious system, Dr. Elie A. Cohen, who had been a prisoner at Auschwitz, considers homosexuality among the inmates as it came under his notice. He thought the shocking environment at first inhibited sexual desire. But, as the prisoners became used to their surroundings, a few were able to arrange their circumstances to permit their involvement in homosexual episodes. Opportunities for this presented themselves only to those who found a certain amount of favor in the eyes of the Nazi overseers, and were thus comparatively free from hunger. As for the rest: "The struggle for existence ... demanded so much of the prisoner's physical energy that he had not enough of it left to worry about sexual matters. Popularly expressed, he had other things to worry about."[6]

Prisoners "in a good state of nutrition," however, found themselves in a position to pay some attention to their sexual needs. These, for the most part, were the camp "prominents", or men who were somehow sheltered from the worst of the camp's brutalities. These men "bought the objects of their love for food, by placing them in less hard labor groups, etc. Federn, who spent a considerable time in Buchenwald, has made a much more positive statement: 'Many German anti-fascists could not resist a handsome boy, so that homosexuality claimed its sacrifice by degrading life and character.' And in *Syntheses* he writes: 'Young men, the camp prostitutes, stalked through the streets and greeted each other with a passing sign ... Love affairs were always developing. Numerous are the couples who, like married people, became inseparable in the most tragic circumstances'." [7]

One is not able to tell, of course, how many of the camp "prominents" were susceptible to homosexual influences before they were confined. The suggestion is made that there were among them anti-fascists "who could not resist a handsome boy." And the description of the young male prostitutes who dispensed their sexual favors in return for that which would lighten the rigors of the camp is an old story to those who know their way about prisons—even the best conducted ones.

A certain number of prisoners in the concentration camps turned to their own sex for relief. Why was this? What happened after they returned to their homes? Were they different from men who experimented homosexually in less brutalizing prisons? Did the homosexual pattern become sufficiently fixed that they will continue to find release with men? As Dr. Cohen points out, hunger prevented most of the prisoners from concerning themselves overmuch with sexual desire. Was it the deprivation of food and the horror inspired by those who had oversight of the place that prevented more men from becoming involved homosexually? Or, by the same token, was the demoralizing atmosphere of the camp a factor in causing men to seek a moment's solace with other men as an antidote to its degradations? Was only the deprivation of conventional sexual outlets important in the making of what one might call "institutional" homosexuals? What *did* make the men in the camps turn to their own sex for relief? Is the difference between these men and the ordinary run of prisoner-turned homosexual one of kind or only of degree? Is there any difference at all? The young hoodlums who are in and out of local jails and reformatories insist that only women interest them sexually. Yet among them are many who, night after night, will accommodate sexually any man who is willing to pay his price.

What is a homosexual? The dictionary definition tells about his sexual propensities. But there are many more things to be considered. As was said in another place, his life is much more than a

chronicle of orgasms. Up to a point, we can describe him. We can
tell what he does. But we are not so sure that we know why he
does these things. There is a long road for us to travel before we
reach a definition of the homosexual that tells more than part of the
story.

Chapter III

SOCIETY IS THE PATIENT

> In its interference with personal conduct, society is seldom thinking of
> anything but the enormity of acting or feeling differently from itself; and this
> standard of judgment, thinly disguised, is held up as the dictate of religion
> and philosophy by nine tenths of all moralists and speculative writers...
> What can the poor public do but apply these instructions and make them their
> personal feelings of good and evil, if they are tolerably unanimous in them,
> obligatory on all the world?"
>
> —*John Stuart Mill*[1]

Ours is a society demanding conformity of its members. It looks
askance at the manners of those whose conduct is at variance with
what is recognized as suitable, and, therefore, good. We are still
fumbling in our efforts to deal realistically with the roles, the rights
and the duties of the few whose thoughts and acts run counter to
what the many unquestioningly accept. Variations from the modes
of expression regarded as the suitable sexual behavior of men are held
to be especially reprehensible. The majority exercises a tyranny over
the minority, and it seeks to repress at least the outward manifestations of nonconformity.

When a homosexual falls upon evil days, he tends to feel that he
is some sort of a scapegoat. The real culprit is society itself. Tolerance is possible only when the tolerated present no threat to the
security of those called upon to exercise it. There are those who feel
that it contains within itself an element of contempt. Certainly
the posturing of a Mexican hairless dog can cause a St. Bernard but a
moment's very minor annoyance. When dissenters seemed dangerous
to the Established Church in England, they were treated with scant
ceremony. Then came the Revolution that chopped off the head of
King Charles the First. When it did its work, it put into the seats
of the mighty those hitherto called the malignants. Then came the
Restoration. Once more the State Church returned to power; and
it kept its erstwhile persecutors well reminded of their dubious state
until the time came when the rule of the bishops seemed impregnable.
Then, and only then, were dissenters left to their own devices. Anyone can practice the virtue of tolerance if the tolerated occasion no
special inconvenience.

The Anglican Church has come to be regarded, both in this country and in England, as the Church of Good Society. Social position and great wealth help its members to look down upon the attenders of meeting houses that lack the blessing of being supervised by bishops. And one supposes that the compliment is returned by those who can take satisfaction out of being holier than the Episcopalians who must "pray out of a book", and whose clergy are sometimes arrayed like Solomon in all his glory.

The conditions of the settlement and expansion of the American Commonwealth made it necessary for the brethren of all shades of theological opinion to dwell together in something approximating tolerance of each other. Despite the fact that this country has had its fair share of theological controversies, no sect has ever enjoyed sufficient power to do very much persecuting for any length of time of those who disagreed with its set of beliefs. It was never possible for an American Torquemada to set up an Inquisition; although there are many who would have tried to do so. Somehow we have learned to live with men of every shade of theological opinion. We manage to find room for them all—from the Fundamentalism of the extreme right to the humanism of the extreme left wing of the Unitarians.

There may be those who see this *laissez-faire* as a sign that the religious fabric is weakening or even becoming moribund. They may feel that no theology has any validity that can afford to admit that it does not contain the sole body of truth. There are those who would be delighted to go to the stake for their religious convictions, and just as delighted to make martyrs of equally devout believers with a different set of convictions. Fortunately, although there are many with the willingness to persecute dissenters from a great variety of orthodoxies, no one in America is able to compel his neighbor to come into the fold.

By and large, we are human enough to like to be rewarded, or at least praised, when we do something meritorious; and we still take into account the belief that punishment comes to those who do evil. It is not at all difficult to understand how the older brother felt in the Parable of the Prodigal Son, when he was obliged to witness the slaying of the fatted calf. He was sure he saw evildoing rewarded: what was the point to being a respectable citizen? Thus the Ten Commandments are statute law, the Sermon on the Mount religion. And we have not yet reached that state of moral excellence where we can afford to dispense with the services of policemen. But, as one considers the proportion of policemen to the number of the population, there is something to be said for the inherent goodness of people.

Society still considers conduct praiseworthy and blameworthy. The good should be rewarded here on earth: this does not happen with sufficient frequency. The chances of the evildoer receiving his come-uppance are somewhat better: at least the prisons are well populated. As Lord Acton tells us, "There is another world for the expiation of guilt; but the wages of folly are payable here below."[2]

So far as one can see, the notion of rewards and punishments is one not likely to be dropped from our thinking for a long time. In our present imperfect state of development, it may not be altogether desirable for society to be without the power to coerce its unruly members. Whether the coercion works is another matter.

We have made quite a bit of progress with those whose behavior we deem criminal, so far as humane treatment is concerned. Even our worst prisons are a bit better than they were twenty years ago. But the prison, which is society's confession of defeat in its attempt to deal with socially deviant behavior, can be an instrument of reformation (whatever that means!) only for those who become convinced that it is desirable to make changes in their mode of living. We still must cope with an army of criminals who see no need for changing their manners or their morals. Convict establishments house many more recidivists than they do first offenders. And what about the misfits—men for whom prison is actually a place of refuge? There are many "good" prison inmates who get into trouble within a very short time after they are let out. This is their way to get back to the place where they are really comfortable. Perhaps they feel secure only behind locked doors, and with someone telling them what to do and when to do it.

Society holds every sane person accountable for what he does. When he offends against the law, he must pay the price. If he is insane, he is placed in a different sort of confinement. The price the court exacts for those it feels are unable to respond to less drastic methods of control is a term in prison. And the length of the term depends upon how the community, through its lawmakers, views the seriousness of the offense. Hitherto no one has questioned the right of the lawmakers to exact penalties that express the indignation of the community for the violation of its felt will. And the law still seeks to make the punishment fit the crime, although there is some talk among penologists about the rehabilitation of criminal offenders. Retribution was out to collect its pound of flesh; and, up to now, there has not been much objection.

But (perhaps as a by-product of the efforts of prison reformers to ameliorate the condition of the inmates of penal institutions), responsible thinkers have begun to question the efficacy of the criminal codes. For one thing, they failed to produce the desired behavior. Fear of a prison sentence has not wiped out crime. It is a commonplace that pickpockets were able to reap a pretty penny cutting the purses of those who congregated to watch a hanging. And capital punishment, which had been the fate destined for those who committed a whole bagful of crimes, fell into such disrepute that juries simply failed to convict. It seems likely that the death sentence, before too long, will be relegated to the chamber of horrors in which are stored the relics of man's inhumanity to man. Putting a man to death for his crimes has never been signally successful as a deterrent.

What sort of substitute society we will be able to devise to take the place of prison is another matter. Furthermore, it is doubtful that we will need to do much thinking about the change for some little time. There will always be a certain number of casualties who, for their own protection as well as that of society, must be kept under lock and key. A start was made long ago when hospitals for the criminally insane were set up. Whether the prison of the future will be an extension of that type of institution, employing different methods and using highly trained personnel, is an interesting exercise that is not quite relevant to what is being discussed in this book.

As far back as 1940, it was advocated that sexual offenders should not be confined in prisons,[3] but should be detained in hospitals until the time when competent medical authority considered them safe to return to the community. This is not a new thing. It had been talked about occasionally, and the notion met with some acceptance in academic and penological circles. The public was not then ready to endorse what was regarded as a revolutionary step. In the *New York Post* of January 6, 1959, there was published what an itinerant reporter found when he undertook to see how the average citizen felt about what society should do with sex offenders. Those questioned were asked whether these men should be kept in a prison or a mental hospital. Four out of five favored confinement in a hospital. Although the sampling is too limited to have very much significance, and remembering that this paper is apt to sit to the left on public questions, the report may still be regarded as having some validity in the search for straws to see how the wind blows.

So far as the law is concerned, the homosexual, when he becomes involved in activity that requires police action, is considered a sex offender. He is of interest to the authorities as a potential criminal, but so is every citizen. Whenever he engages in intimacy with another male, he commits a crime and is liable to arrest and imprisonment.

Homosexuals are under special disabilities with respect to the law enforcement authorities. It is said that when a homosexual is undesirably discharged from the Armed Forces the local police are notified. Thus he is a marked man in his home community or in whatever place he proposes to settle. In at least one state, men convicted of homosexual offenses are required to register with the police in whatever town they may reside. Men discharged from the service because of homosexuality have found it impossible to obtain employment in occupations where Government clearance is required. One man, who had devoted a lifetime in preparation for a highly specialized craft, found himself unable to work at his trade because many years previously he had told his superiors in the Army he was afraid he might get into trouble because of his homosexual tendencies and wanted help. He was discharged without honor within a month. He is still paying for believing an Army chaplain's statement: "If anything is troubling you, come and see me about it."

The number of disabilities under which a homosexual labors in addition to serving time in prison and undesirable extrusion from the armed forces seem out of proportion to what might be regarded as his offensive conduct. His so-called debt to society is not considered paid in full when the prison doors close after him or when he is drummed out of the service. A student would do well to devote a volume to the effect these social penalties, discriminations, hostilities and rejections have on the personalities of those who must live with them.

The homosexual must take into account what we called the unholy trinity of fears: of the police, of exposure, and of the blackmailer.‘ How anyone could make anything like a good adjustment under the circumstances is difficult to comprehend. The situation is not too different, as has been observed, from that of men and women of any political, social, racial, religious, or even faddist, minority. Yet there are some who insist that unpleasant things that happen to members of groups such as these are self caused and that there is little that can be done about it. It has been said that society itself is the patient.

The community has been slow to accept its share of responsibility for making what must be regarded as casualties of the social order. Occasionally it sets up standards that are unworkable. The Prohibition Law is an excellent case in point. Although most of us feel that theft is inherently evil, we have come to learn that the thief is not altogether a free agent when he steals. Most of our criminal courts have probation departments whose duty it is to investigate the histories of men convicted of crime. They seek to discover the reasons and the roots of the crime that brought its perpetrator before the court, and an effort is made to uncover the factors that made him what he is. This is done so that the offense may be understood in relation to him who committed it. Such an exploration represents a distinct departure from the punitive philosophy hitherto governing the imposition of sentences. In the case of the homosexual offender, where doubt has been thrown on the right of society to imprison men for the outward manifestation of the attraction of two adults for each other, the situation becomes more complicated.

Judges required to sentence men for homosexual offenses may be in somewhat the same position as were the courts when it became increasingly clear that the Prohibition Amendment was in its last days and that repeal could be expected momentarily. It became indubitable that the sentiment of the American people as a whole was very much against locking up minor traffickers in illicit liquor. Today considerable doubt has arisen with respect to the unanimity of general public belief in the soundness of the law that puts two adults in prison for what they do in private. As it stands, the police force would have to be augmented to unbelievable proportions if any serious attempt were made to arrest all who were involved in homosexual acts in the course of one night. Admittedly there is a very different opinion with respect to those who offend against the young, the unwilling, or those unable to take care of themselves through physical or mental incapacity. And society must have a great deal of control over those who make nuisances of themselves in public places. The Wolfenden Report shows unmistakably that a highly representative section of enlightened public opinion feels the time has come for changes to be made in the penal laws.

In 1939 a predecessor of the George W. Henry Foundation sought to discover the views on the problem of homosexuality held by community leaders in and around the city of New York. One hundred persons of more than average standing were approached to answer questions as to what they thought society should do about the matter. Approximately five-sixths of those approached sent replies. The questionnaire sought answers from a carefully selected group—clergymen, social workers, judges, probation officials, penologists, physicians, psychiatrists, psychologists and suchlike—who were asked how they viewed the homosexual. They were requested to address themselves to the possibility of his being a sick person in need of treatment, a criminal, an undesirable citizen, or simply one who should be regarded as a productive but somewhat different member of society. And they were asked to tell what they thought should be done about the homosexual. Should he be imprisoned, helped to obtain treatment, adjured to change his ways, or simply let alone? A very large majority of those questioned were of opinion that homosexuals were sick persons in need of treatment. Two were certain that he was a criminal; these were a police official and the head of a society for the suppression of vice. One or two respondents, who normally could be counted upon to take an extremely tolerant view of anything that involved the right of the individual to go his way with a minimum of interference, thought that the homosexual was not in parlous state. As to what should be done about the problem most of those who responded to the questionnaire were of opinion that psychiatric help should be brought to bear. The same two who considered the homosexual to be criminal naturally felt that he should be imprisoned. And three individuals were equally certain that homosexuals were best left to their own devices.

This is how an intelligent group of individuals viewed the picture more than twenty years ago. It does not seem possible that many changes have taken place in the minds of liberal men and women since that time. If there is any change, it would seem to be in the direction of greater liberality of opinion. None the less, one wonders whether even this enlightened group, all of whom signed their names to what they had written in reply to the questionnaire, might not have cocked the fraction of a weather eye in the direction of caution. And one wonders what they would have said at the time of the furor when a United States Senator was able to stand the country on its ears for a while with his discovery that there were homosexuals and even Communists who managed to find jobs for themselves in a most sedate Government office.

Certainly to-day there is more feeling that there is something amiss in society's treatment of the homosexual than there was at the outbreak of the Second World War. Of this we have some clue when even an occasional policeman can be heard to say that "there is something the matter" with a homosexual, and that society should find something more intelligent to do with him than putting him in jail.

To continue in this fashion is simply to state and re-state the obvious. All it does is to labor what everyone knows, or ought to know, but does precious little to correct. To go on in this strain brings us dangerously near to the fallacy of regarding homosexuality as an end in itself. More likely it is the manifestation of a larger social problem. In the case of the individual, Dr. Henry points out that it is a symptom of a deep-seated personality conflict.[5] In the case of society, Dr. Bailey states emphatically that the problem of homosexuality is the problem of a sick society. Thus he shows us that the real culprit is society itself:

"In any society the extent of homosexual practice and perversion is always one of the more striking indications of a general corruption or defect of its sexual life. To-day the so-called 'problem of homosexuality' which confronts us is really a problem arising from the decay of moral standards and the abandonment of moral responsibility in the field of heterosexual relations—both, in their turn, the result of false and imperfect conceptions of the nature of sex, and of ignorance or rejection of the will of God for men and women. Homosexual perversion, therefore, is not itself a fount of corrupting influence, but only, as it were, the ineluctable consequence of a corrosion which has already left its mark upon marriage and family life and, if not checked, may ultimately undermine the social order and lead to sexual anarchy. Consequently any attempt to suppress homosexual practices by the rigour of the criminal law is merely a feeble attempt to cure symptoms while neglecting the disease that produced them. Despite what may seem at times to be almost an attitude of complacent indifference to its condition, there is little doubt that our society is aware of the nature of this disease, and that it has at bottom a profoundly uneasy conscience on that score. But, sooner or later, an unpalatable truth must be faced: Instead of addressing itself energetically to all that is amiss in its sexual life and ideas, it has attempted to relieve its sense of guilt by turning on the male homosexual as a convenient scape-goat. Such a projection of blame is, of course, ultimately futile; but much distress, harm, and injustice may be caused before it can be ultimately exposed as a discreditable evasion of responsibility."[6]

Even though we may be persuaded that the responsibility for the unsatisfactory position of the homosexual is due to society itself, there is still a great deal that can be done, here and now, to make the load of individual homosexuals somewhat less burdensome. Society may be sick, but it is not incurable. What is thought by the community has a great deal to do with the untenable situation in

which the homosexual finds himself; but little is accomplished if we
simply lay the burden of sin upon a new scapegoat, society, and call
it a day.

The homosexual, it is said, is what he is through no deliberate
act or choice of his own: therefore he should not be penalized when
he runs foul of the law. This sort of specious reasoning can be used
to extricate any sort of criminal from the consequences of his acts.
And it looks suspiciously like our becoming embroiled in the old
philosophical quarrel between freedom and determinism. If what
we do is preordained, then we have no choice in the matter. Therefore it is a cruel society that punishes us for what we do that is amiss;
we were fated to do what we ought not to have done. And, if we do
have complete freedom of choice with respect to what we do, then
we must accept the full responsibility for the consequences of our
actions. To this the only answer that seems to make any sense is
Kant's compromise—we are partly free and partly determined. A
society in which no one is required to regard the consequences of his
behavior would be an unthinkable place. The homosexual who feels
that everything he does is beyond his power to control or modify
lives in a fool's paradise. Too many feel no sense of responsibility;
they are persuaded that their attempts to seek the good life are
futile. Some have been so conditioned that they feel that nothing
matters. They are sure that society will condemn them without a
hearing.

Here Peter Wildeblood comes to our rescue. As we view what
happened to him at the hands of a social order that made no particular attempt to understand his situation when he fell upon evil
days, we are tempted to wonder whether, in his case, imprisonment
might not have served a useful purpose. Did the mature reflection
he exhibits in his book come as the result of what he endured in
order to satisfy society's demand for its pound of flesh? Would he
have written so thoughtfully had he not been imprisoned? Societ
has charged a high price for the privilege of being able to read this
testament of courage in the time of adversity. Out of what Mr.
Wildeblood learned while he was in prison, he was able to say that:

"It has become the fashion in recent years to blame Society almost
exclusively for the existence of its misfits. The prostitute, the burglar
and the delinquent child are not, we are told, deliberately choosing
to go wrong—the choice is imposed upon them by the civilization
into which they have been born. 'Society,' it is said, 'gets the criminals
it deserves,' and it has been said, too, that society gets the homo-

sexuals it deserves. It seems to me that such generalisations are only partly true; it is in the interaction between society and its failures, in their effect upon and their attitudes toward each other, that the answers to these problems will be found.'"

The genius of the Anglo-Saxon society consists in part of the gradualness with which it embarks upon social change. That has been able to prevent many bloody upheavals. The emancipation of the Negro takes a great many years to accomplish; and the process is still going on. Society hopes that its institutions are permanent, and social changes are always viewed with considerable skepticism. Save for the few who are devoted to change for change's sake, the majority of Britons and Americans are content to plod along with the machinery that does a fairly good job. Like the Old Time Religion in the Gospel song, they are apt to feel that if

"It was good enough for my father,
"It's good enough for me."

But change is inevitable. It took quite a bit of effort for the inhabitants of this planet to accept the fact that the earth is round, and the Church strove valiantly to delay the world's acceptance of the fact. Perhaps the two most conservative forces that hold our civilization together are the law and the church. Ordinarily one would not expect lawyers and theologians to unite to press for new ways of dealing with the sexually deviated; more often than not they do their best to postpone anything that makes for change of the tried and true ways of doing things. Strangely enough, authoritative voices among lawyers and churchmen have been raised to insist that society re-examine its responsibility for those it had hitherto cast into outer darkness. The demand for the appointment of the Wolfenden Commission was pressed most strongly by a group within the Church of England—its Moral Welfare Council.

There is a great temptation to indulge in a bit of prophecy about the shape of things to come. Donning the prophet's mantle, however, carries its own difficulties; and one should be more than a bit cautious. The prediction may safely be ventured that, sooner or later, public support of the recommendations of the Wolfenden Commission will make Parliament aware that the people view the matter of penal legislation against homosexuals somewhat differently than they have done in the past; and ultimately the Commission's recommendations will become the law of the land. Still later the proposals of the American Law Institute, which are substantially the same as those of Sir John Wolfenden and his colleagues, will find their way into the American statute books. This may take somewhat longer; because intrenched power in this country resists social changes that may tend to weaken moral sanctions more honored in the breach than in the observance, but must, for the sake of proprieties, remain in the pasture where the sacred cows graze.

Nor need it be expected that this desirable outcome will come about immediately; it will take quite some time. The opposition to the Wolfenden Report in the House of Lords is quite vocal, and perhaps powerful. The peers objected to any relaxation of the severity of the penal laws, because they feared that lessening the severity of punishment would loose a horde of sex criminals upon the country. This sort of argument is always taken out of mothballs when proposals are put forward to abolish capital punishment. If society fails to execute its murderers, then, they claim, no one is safe in his bed; and human life will be so cheap that everyone will take potshots at the man next door. Ingrained fears of mitigation of the penalties of the law are always utilized by those who believe that crimes were properly dealt with in the good old days, when capital punishment was available to dispose of children who did that which today would bring them only a warning. So far as statistics have any meaning, there is no noticeable increase in homicides in the American states that have abolished the death penalty for murder.

Despite the fact that we are morally certain that we cannot legislate men into righteousness, we act as though we could. To expect the homosexual to desist from conduct that he feels to be an integral part of himself is a vain expectation. Even though he is aware of what will happen if he is caught, he will go on taking his chances. This was true when men faced the possibility of being executed for participation in a homosexual offense. There is no reason to believe that the likelihood of a term in jail will keep men from seeking and finding those equally prepared to take chances to fulfil themselves, as they see it.

There was a doctrine in the civil law that men engaged in hazardous occupations assumed the risk of accidents as a necessary incident of their employment. This theory of assumed risk prevented injured workmen from recovering damages when they sued to recoup themselves for their sufferings in an industrial accident. The enactment of the Workmen's Compensation Laws put an end to the employers' defence that, because the injured workman knew a job to be dangerous to life or limb, he could not collect damages. The law held that those who engaged in hazardous jobs knew the conditions there-

of, and accepted them as something to be borne in order to make a
living. The passage of the workmen's compensation act was fought
to the last ditch by the die-hards. As workmen engaged in hazardous
trades were obliged to accept the risks involved in that type of work,
so, one supposes, the homosexual must accept the hazards of arrest,
exposure, and the attentions of the blackmailer as part of the assumed
risk of being a homosexual. As the courts held that injured workmen knew what they were doing when they took jobs that were
productive of accidents, so the homosexual may be assumed to take
on the risks that accompany the hazardous search for sexual companionship. And it is equally certain that the die-hards will resist
changes that reduce the hazards for the homosexual who hopes that
a kindly-disposed society might be induced to make the world a little
safer for him.

It is not altogether easy to account for the forces that are intent
to block progress toward the emancipation of the homosexual. Not
all of the advocates for repression come to court with the same set
of motives. It is comparatively easy to understand those who resist
all manner of change—whether it be in the traditional manner of
using a knife and fork or minor changes in the high school curriculum,
or whether, like Queen Victoria, they fear the world would be on its
way to perdition if an enlisted man were permitted to grow a beard.
It is also easy to see how some might look upon the emancipation of
the homosexual as a threat to their own security. They could quite
easily resent others being permitted to do what they feared to do.
One irreverent soul suggested that the psychiatrists who advocated
the retention of the Draconian laws might have a special axe to
grind. Would patients continue to come flocking to them for treatment? Would they feel it necessary to be cured of what would no
longer be against the law?

Here is our difficulty. It has been suggested that society itself must
bear some responsibility for the homosexual's plight. We speak of
society and the homosexual as though they were two separate entities.
But are they? Society is composed of all sorts and conditions of men,
with all sorts of problems arising out of varying types of sexual adjust-
ments and their lack. To speak of the homosexual as though he existed
apart from the rest of the body social, even though he may be made to
feel so, is to do violence to the facts. One of the greatest stumbling
blocks that all of us must surmount when we attempt to study any
maladjusted group is our unwillingness to accept the ineluctable
fact that society must be viewed as a whole. The sexually maladjust-

ed are part of the social whole. To regard them as something other (and all of us do this to some degree) is to miss the point entirely.

It takes all kinds of human beings to constitute a society—saints and sinners, sick and well, honest and dishonest, rich and poor, haves and have-nots. No matter how many gestures of exclusion the haves may make, they cannot ignore the presence of the have-nots. Nor, no matter how much this may seem desirable to the haves, can problems of the have-nots fail to exercise their attention. For the whole is greater than its parts, and the have-nots are a part of the whole. Although, as Disraeli put it,[8] there is only one war in the world—the war between the haves and have-nots—the war is not always fought on the open field of battle. Sometimes there are long periods of uneasy peace. As Peter Wildeblood sees it, "Each community consists of two opposed groups: the majority, whose beliefs dictate the customs, and whose members accept its rules without questioning them, and the minority which, often violently, rejects these rules and creates an underworld of its own. Between the conformists and the rebels lies the no-man's land."[9]

Thus is stated the rules for the civil war within every society. It is an unequal struggle, because the majority who make the rules can enforce them through the exercise of naked power. Fortunately few homosexuals are at war with those who make the rules all of the time. Many are able to live relatively untroubled lives. It is only in time of crisis that they are made painfully conscious of the war between themselves and the social order. And society, in its turn, is relatively untroubled by the presence of the homosexual in its midst until an untoward event creates a need for a scapegoat who can be dealt with unpleasantly with a minimum of trouble. Occasionally some politican or sensation monger can use him as a whipping boy, when he is without something better to utilize to show his constituents that he is the terror of evildoers. Until yesterday, so to speak, homosexuals feared to fight back. From the West Coast have come some militant publications and a national organization has been formed to combat the prejudices that can be used by the unscrupulous to bring hardship to sexual nonconformists.

That these prejudices are deep-rooted is obvious. What can be done to rid ourselves of them? How should we go about reconsidering what sexual conduct is acceptable, and what is not to be tolerated? For one thing, it is necessary that the community be in possession of much more reliable information concerning the causes and conditions of sexual deviation than the average citizen, or, for that matter, the

individual otherwise well informed, has in possession. Much has
been done here; but the scholars have only begun to scratch the
surface. Even with the limitations upon our knowledge, there is
more that can be done here and now to help men who have fallen
upon evil days, or who may desire to come to better terms with
themselves and with the social order.

The community has another responsibility. It must accept its
moral obligation to help those of its members who fall short of the
standards it sets for social self-sufficiency. Those who are unable
to carry their own weight impoverish it in varying degrees. In self-
protection, society must re-examine the stand it has taken, so that
every member thereof is in a position to make his full contribution
of productiveness. In recent years, the problem of homosexuality
has been regarded as one of mental health. For that reason, the
psychiatrists have taken the lead in research and treatment. Of
necessity they will require a great deal of help. The approach to the
problem has well been described as a multi-disciplinary one. Perhaps a great deal of money should be spent for research; but no matter
how costly any project for the betterment of needy human beings may
be, it will be much less than what society spends for maintaining
homosexuals who have fallen by the wayside in prisons and mental
hospitals.

The public discussion of the problem of homosexuality serves at
least one useful end. It brings to homosexuals themselves the knowledge that they are not alone, and that there are those who exhibit a
genuine concern for their welfare. They may learn, thus, that it is
possible to receive help to cope with the desires and compulsions they
fear. And it is quite possible that some youngsters may be saved
from an unwholesome adolescence if it were made clear to them
that the homosexual experimentation of the very young might well
be included in the catalogue of growing pains. If those thus troubled
are enabled to find persons and places where they might bring their
problems in the hope of sound advice rather than moral lectures and
pious admonitions to avoid the occasion of sin, then it is well that the
knowledge be made widespread that homosexual behavior is more pre-
valent than has been hitherto acknowledged.

It has yet to be determined whether homosexuality is, as one
psychiatrist expressed it, a disease or a way of life. This much is
certain. If homosexuals are sick people, then there must be a better
way of treating them than by locking them up in prison cells. It is
a long time since society abandoned that method of treating the

mentally ill, although vestiges of it still survive here and there. In any case, there is a strong feeling abroad that society has not done too well in its treatment of those whose sexual behavior differs from that of the majority.

Thus far, the only answer to the problem of homosexuality has been repression. It gave respectability to that way of solving a minority problem by calling it criminal justice. Such a solution is hoary with disreputable old age. The Spanish Inquisition employed all the forms of legality to justify what it tried to do. So, for that matter, did Hitler.

Times change. Beliefs once held binding upon all men become less absolute as they are seen to run counter to what actually happens in the world around us. Doubtless there was a time when society believed the homosexual to possess a very real threat to its security. The belief still persists. And it has many supporters, some of whom sit in high places. But it is high time to discard the view that the homosexual's conduct excludes him from the protection of the community. Certainly many responsible leaders in the churches and responsible workers in the sciences feel that such a view should be relegated to the limbo of forgotten dogmas.

Socrates called himself a gadfly. He deemed it his duty to stand in the market place and ask inconvenient questions. He insisted that his fellow Athenians re-examine many of the ideas that time had sanctified and that nobody troubled to question. Has not the time come for modern gadflies to pose some inconvenient questions with respect to the standards of sexual morality our modern world regards as sacrosanct? Whence came they? Who decided that they were above criticism? Who made it appear sacrilegious to inquire into their meaning and validity? Is the ultimate seat of authority the power of society to enforce its will upon those who think differently from the majority?

Those who work to bring about the Good Society see its members as free men who walk in the light of reason. With St. Paul, they "prove all things and hold fast to that which is good."[10] Moral excellence is not attained by coercing a people into thinking what their betters decide is good for them.

Chapter IV

THE MATTER OF TREATMENT

To attain any assured knowledge of the soul is one
of the most difficult things in this world.

—Aristotle[1]

Several years ago, a psychiatrist devoted a book to the consideration of whether homosexuality was a disease or a way of life. Those who believe that the homosexual's behavior is normal for him do not tend to be interested in the possibilities of treatment. As a matter of fact, the treatment of homosexuals is not regarded by the experts with anything like unanimity. Moreover, although there are external evidences of the manifestations of homosexuality, there is no definition thereof, save in the most general terms. There are a variety of ways by which we can approach the definition of homosexuality. The physicians look at it one way, the psychologists in another, the social scientists in still a third way; to the clergy it is something else again, and so on. It is certain that, although the scientists have discovered some of the causes and conditions of homosexuality, they are not in a position to say with authority, "Here is what we can put our finger on; this is it!" We know much more about the phenomena of homosexuality than we do about its etiology.

Today the opinion is fairly general that homosexuals are in need of help. But, as there is no universally held opinion as to cause, so, likewise, there is no agreement as to how it can best be treated. By and large, it is fairly generally assumed that treatment is to be conducted in terms of what is called psychotherapy. This is defined by Dr. Henry in *All the Sexes*: "Psychotherapy is a method of treatment which aims at discovering modifying and eliminating the emotional factors in illness so that the patient may be able to adjust to reality wi th self-assurance and satisfaction, and without dependence on neurotic symptoms. It is a loosely used term. Its virtues are frequently overrated, and the results sometimes claimed for it can be related to quackery and magic. A few of its principles antedate historic medicine; they have their origin in primitive magic and religious practices. Illness, both physical and mental, was originally believed to be the result of the activities of superhuman beings who must be placated, and of maleficent spirits who must be exorcised by means of charms, rites and incantations."

The persistence of the view that psychiatrists are the lineal descendants of primitive witch doctors can be seen in the modern facetious reference to them as head shrinkers. So far as the sexual deviations are concerned, the psychiatrists came fairly late on the scene. In the past, the phenomena of sexual deviations were discussed as though they were (and there are some who, to this day, think they are) the preoccupation of the clergy and the servants of the law. Sexual behavior was regarded as an ethical and legal problem. Was the conduct under question right or wrong? When the social and medical sciences began to poach on the territory staked out by the conservators of the law and theology, the emphasis changed.[2] The physicians were interested in curing illness, the social scientists in correcting maladjustments. The scientific viewpoint was said to be oblivious of moral considerations. With the exception of the normative study of ethics, which not too long ago was called moral philosophy, scientific method was supposed to limit itself to matters of intellectual correctness. There are students of ethics who regard their task as fulfilled when they present descriptions of what they observe. They view themselves in the same light as the psychologists or anthropologists, who report what they find and leave the conclusions for others to draw. The notion of scientific method contemplates behavior as something to be studied empirically. Ordinarily it is not prone to lend itself to the support of moral presuppositions or the making of value judgements.

One of the reasons why the older type of theologian distrusted his psychiatric opposite number was fear that the psychiatrist might be, if not immoral, at least amoral. In respect to the homosexual, the psychiatrist is confronted with what Bernard Shaw called the doctor's dilemma. He is apt to be in similar case to that of the physician who is called upon to treat a luetic patient. Has the physician the right to consult his prejudices against men with syphilis? He may consider it a nasty business; he may regard its victim as a sinful person; he may even go so far as to consider him a loathsome individual. All these things he may think; but, once having accepted the man as a patient, he is duty bound, no matter what he thinks, to employ his best efforts to cure his patient—for doctors are concerned with the business of ridding the community of a carrier of infection. So, when a sexually deviated patient comes to the psychiatrist's office, it is unimportant, once he is permitted to stay, how the doctor views his morals. The doctor is there to cure the sick.[3] However, there is no compulsion on the part of the psychiatrist to accept all who knock at his door. Both doctor and patient have free choice—the patient to choose his doctor and the doctor to take or leave the patient. Once a sexually maladjusted individual is accepted for treatment, the doctor would seem to place himself under obligation to promote his patient's best welfare. It is not the function of the doctor to take his patient to task for his moral derelictions, or augment his burden of culpability by employing threats and menaces. Moral lectures and admonitions for the delinquent to mend their ways doubtless have their place; but that place is not in the course of psychiatric treatment. Yet, by the same token, the psychiatrist must help a maladjusted individual to come to terms with himself and the world in which he lives. This is also part of the doctor's dilemma.

In the terms of our present day civilization, the homosexual is a maladjusted individual. Adjustment has been defined as the adaptation, preferably the successful adaption, of an individual to his environment.[4] The environment our Anglo-Saxon society calls good contemplates marriage as well as the establishment of a home and founding of a family. Departures from this norm are generally regarded with varying degrees of disapproval. The term one sometimes hears—old maids of both sexes—gives an idea of how society views those who fail to fall into the pattern of sexual conformity.

All maladjustments seem to carry with themselves a certain amount of social stigma. There are still some who equate illness with immorality. Who of us, having acquired a common cold, has not been reproached by one or another of his women-folk for not wearing rubbers? The mental illnesses had to be kept out of sight. To have a relative in a mental hospital, or, as it was called in the old days, an insane asylum, was considered disgraceful. There are still sections of opinion that consider mental illness and criminality somehow related.

Nor are we without those who feel that poverty is the result of thriftlessness, if not downright crime. They are convinced that the poor are to blame for their plight. The spirit of the Elizabethan poor laws will take a long time dying. There are preachers who justify harsh treatment of the poor by suggesting that it is impossible for a good man to be poor. They have a proof text from the Psalms to reinforce their views: "I have not seen the righteous forsaken or his children begging bread."[5] If all this is true of the mentally ill and the poor whose condition, at least on the surface, carries no stigma of sexual misconduct, how much more condemnatory is the attitude of persons of this type of mind toward the sexually deviated! When a homosexual reaches the psychiatrist, treatment can be made just that more difficult because the patient labors under a cloud never wholly to be dispelled—for no man can completely separate himself from the world's opinion. And the psychiatrist is perforce obliged to help his patient live with what the world thinks about him and those like him.

Let us look once more at the definition of adjustment in which we call it the adaptation of the individual to his environment. To help a homosexual to a satisfactory adjustment, he must be brought into the most favorable possible relation to the world of which he is a part. This may mean that he must revise his view of himself as part of the social order. He may have to be re-educated to manage more effectively his work, his social life, his play, and the occasions in which he temporarily merges his individuality into the activity of one or another group. As the patient is helped to do this, he can be said to be on the way to a more satisfactory adjustment.

How accomplish this? Here there is no unanimity. There are physicians who feel that the complete transformation of the homosexual into something quite different is the outcome to be desired. There are times, however, when what appears on the surface to be a wholly desirable result can make a "reformed" homosexual into something quite unpleasant to contemplate. Sinners who forsake what they consider their evil ways may find it necessary to spend hours in condemning their companions of former days. They are not unlike the prostitute who has managed to work her way into the ranks of the respectable, and who finds it necessary to join the unhappy throng of those members of society who condemn her sisters of her more colorful existence.

There are doctors who feel that all homosexuals do best when they undergo transformation. When Peter Wildeblood was seen in prison by a psychiatrist and asked about treatment that would change his way of life, he asked whether what happened under therapy might not make him into another sort of person.[*] He was told that this might be the case. The psychiatrist put it to him quite properly that he must take this seriously into account before he decided to embark upon the radical treatment that might change him from a homosexual into something else. There are also doctors who view some homosexuals as "valuable and efficient members of the community, quite unlike the common conception of the homosexual as being necessarily, or probably, vicious, criminal, effete, or depraved."[*]

The psychiatrist who undertakes the treatment of a homosexual is confronted with a third dilemma. What should be its guiding prin-

ciple? Should he remake the patient into what he thinks the moral
sense of the community demands? How much should he consult the
patient's own view of his needs, even though he fears that this will
make for a tragic outcome? What of the doctor's conception of the
place of the homosexual in the social order? Can he avoid being influenced by this? Here we can only propose some uncomfortable
questions. This is not the place to suggest answers that only the
keepers of the psychiatrists' consciences can supply.

It is axiomatic, however, that the doctor-patient relationship is a
moral one. No patient resorts to a physician save to be helped.
And patients would do well to heed Chesterton's advice to London
landladies to be more particular about what a prospective tenant
thought about God than the state of his pocketbook. The Chesterton-
ian paradox has more than a little applicability to the homosexual
seeking help. Sometimes his whole pattern of life may be changed
through his commerce with the doctor: therefore he seems entitled to
have some knowledge of how the doctor's mind works. Yet, by
the same token, what self-respecting phychiatrist dare promise a
man who comes to him for treatment more than his best efforts?

The person who suffers from the ordinary run of malady is best
served if he is passive in the doctor's hands. If he has a cold, he will
be expected to go to bed, take fruit juices and whatever medicine
is given him, and stay there until the doctor tells him to take up his
bed and walk. The man with a sexual difficulty, if he hopes to get
well, is required to participate actively in the cure. Too frequently
has it been observed that patients with this sort of problem would
like to act as though they had a bad cold and let the doctor do all
the work. They want to be completely passive. The situation is not
that simple.

Again we turn to the definition of adjustment which calls it the
adaptation to an environment. One has to get along, somehow, with a
world from which escape is impossible. Implicit in the business of
getting along is a learning process. Unfortunately the doctor cannot
give his patient a course of lectures, expect him to take copious
notes, pass an examination, and be sent out into the world with a
diploma certifying that his troubles are over. Before the patient can
reach that advantageous state, he will have to submit to an exploration that will uncover more than he ever thought could be learned
about himself. Strengthened by what he is able to learn, the patient
should be equipped to go out into the world and meet whatever

the fates have in store for him with a great deal more equanimity than when he came for help.

The acquisition of self-knowledge is a slow and painful process. Some psychiatrists prefer to confine the treatment to a simple doctor-patient relationship. Some require the services of psychologists to conduct tests that reveal facets of the patient's personality that are not only time-saving short cuts but also serve as checks upon the doctor's own observations. In other cases, the psychiatrist might be considered the captain of a team that would include the psychologist, a psychiatric social worker, and perhaps a clergyman. There are therapists who feel that the patient will get the best results if drastic changes are made in his environment. Sometimes it is felt that the patient would profit from a new place of residence and a job which would afford him a better chance to be himself. And there are doctors who go so far as to help the patient seek and find associates and friends who seem better suited to meet his need for newer ways of thinking and living.

The treatment process can sometimes be so far-reaching in its results that the patient is quite right to inquire whether it might not be an actual attempt to create a totally new personality. But, just as the plastic surgeon can make a man a new face, no matter what changes may be effected in one's mode of thinking and acting, the same person must continue to think and act. New wine is being poured into old bottles. Unless there is a very real desire on the patient's part to co-operate, he is not apt to derive much benefit from it.

What can a patient hope to gain from psychiatric treatment? What assurance has he that treatment will help him better his condition? What sort of treatment holds some promise of a successful outcome? How long will it take? How much will it cost? What sort of persons are qualified to treat homosexuals? How does one find out how good a therapist might be? Should one change his doctor if he finds that he is not being helped? All of these questions are pertinent to be asked by a person contemplating making changes in his mode of life under psychiatric care.[8]

No one in his right mind would undertake to propose answers to these questions that would apply to everyone. One of the great principles to be followed is that every patient is an end in himself, and he presents a set of problems that are peculiarly his. The experience of others can be a helpful guide. No psychiatrist worthy of the name will set up a bed of Procrustes into which every patient must fit, and either chop off his head or stretch him out until, comfortably or uncomfortably, he fits into a set of preconceptions about what is to be done with those who fall into a particular category. Any answers to the questions propounded here are highly tentative and general in their implications. While they might be suitable for a large number of homosexual patients, they contain within themselves the limitations inherent in all generalizations.

In the first place, homosexuals, when they consider psychotherapy usually think in terms of being cured. Cure may be taken to mean such a complete change in the patient's mode of living that he will as a result thereof, find his sexual satisfactions with women. From this type of treatment, he expects to change his mode of sexual expression so that he can behave in ways that commend themselves to the social order. He expects to gain proficiency and satisfaction from conventional modes of sexual activity. More than that, he is hopeful that treatment will bring him not only physical but also emotional gratification, and a sense of fulfillment as well. As a result of successful treatment, he hopes to be able to marry, have children and found a family.

Let there be no mistake about the matter. Such a programme involves the expenditure of a good bit of blood, sweat and tears. In another place, it is likened unto the heroic treatment of drug addiction called "cold turkey," which leaves the patient to sweat it out as best he can. Of course the psychiatrist is there to give support when the going is rough; and he is ready to pick up the pieces when the patient stumbles, and even falls. Many times during the course of the treatment the patient may go forward for a while, only to slip back to the place where he is sometimes ready to throw in the sponge. There is no royal road to making a homosexual into something else.

Although it seems necessary to point out the difficulties that must be met by one who seeks to make these radical changes in his mode of living, it is possible to look at the other side of the coin. Many psychiatrists have some admirable results to their credit. In many instances, the cure seems to be permanent in its effects. We know of some lasting as long as twenty years. Occasionally one hears of a man who does very well under treatment: under great stress he might fall into a homosexual episode. These lapses seem to make very little difference in the assessment of the total personality. None the less, a single detected slip could mean the undoing of years of treatment. A man can "stay on the wagon" (as the phrase goes with relation to the alcoholic) for maybe ten years. Then, under some especially harrowing circumstances, he may resort to what he basically disapproves. It is not pleasant to contemplate the harm thus done.

Sometimes the psychiatrist is able to give substantial relief to the patient who is not prepared to take the vigorous steps necessary to acquire a completely new mode of existence. Such an individual can be helped to "live with his neurosis", as this is currently being talked about. Where this is the treatment of choice, the patient is helped to a realistic stock-taking, and he is encouraged to attain the strengths that will enable him to control the hectic search for sexual companionship that he might hitherto have thought so necessary. This, too, is progress.

Answering the first question in the most general terms it would appear that psychotheraphy can successfully abort a homosexual way of life and help the patient to make the changes whereby he can find sexual satisfaction in the socially approved ways of deriving it. This is what is commonly regarded as cure. In comparison with the number of cases seen by psychiatrists the number of reported cures is quite small. The patient has a right to hope for such an outcome, but he must be prepared to realize that the road thereto is not easy. Less revolutionary changes are relatively easy to bring about, and the condition of almost any homosexual can be relieved to help him function with a minimum of discomfort.

The answer to the second question is much more optimistic than what can be said in reply to the first. Practically everyone can benefit from psychotherapy, if only from supportive treatment in time of crisis. It is the rare homosexual who comes away from treatment without some measure of improvement, even though he may be reluctant to admit it. No one loves a benefactor. When someone came to Al Smith and told him that a ward politician whom he had once befriended was going around telling all and sundry how vile he was, the Man in the Brown Derby scratched his head for a moment and said, "I wish I could remember what I did for *him*."

The third question—the one relating to the sort of treatment that gives promise of a successful outcome—is one that does not lie within the competence of this book. Those best qualified to answer it would be the psychiatrists themselves; but here one must enter a *caveat*. Any psychiatrist worth his salt would say that the the therapeutic methods he employs are the best possible ones. Dr. Henry suggests that he utilizes such modifications of the method of psychoanalysis as seem suitable for the need of the patient. It would seem to be the general impression that psychoanalysis in some form is the type of therapy that offers the greatest measure of hope.

No one can say with any degree of assurance how long treatment will take. From what a layman can see, one should count on spending at least a year with the doctor, and it is doubtful that very much can be accomplished in so little time. A little reflection should convince those interested that a condition of ten or twenty years' standing cannot be relieved in a month or two—much less eradicated.

The cost of treatment varies with the psychiatrists who fix the fees for their services. Frankly the expense is great. Unlike the general practitioner, the psychiatrist can see only a limited number of patients in the course of a day, and the number of hours he can devote to his work depend upon his powers of endurance. By and large, the private services of a psychiatrist can be engaged only by those who have the wherewithal. Moderately circumstanced patients can resort to fee-charging clinics, and there are public and voluntary hospital services to which those without means can resort. Unfortunately these last are overcrowded. Save in dire emergency, where places like Bellevue Hospital Psychiatric Division are way stations to state institutions for the mentally ill, the medically indigent will meet difficulty in obtaining treatment.

The question of who may treat homosexuals, or those milder forms of mental aberrations not requiring hospitalization, is a moot one. Legally any licensed physician may treat any form of illness. Usually it is recommended that the physician who treats mental illness be a qualified psychiatrist. Clinical psychologists can and do treat persons suffering from mental dysfunctions. More recently, clinically trained clergymen have undertaken the pastoral counselling of homosexuals, and these specially trained men are doing remarkably fine work. In the short time that the clinical training movement has been in operation in the churches, it has more than justified its existence. It gives promise of increased usefulness, and, better still, it opens a new resource to those unable to pay the fees of private physicans, and whose situation is such that they prefer not to resort to public facilities. With the dearth of psychiatrists and the limited resources of many patients in need of long-term treatment, the use of trained ancillary personnel is becoming more widespread. Thus is treatment in one form or another made available for all.

Only fools rush in where angels fear to tread. For a layman to venture an opinion as to how good a psychiatrist might be is to make a judgment for which he lacks the criteria. Doubtless it is possible to obtain information about the esteem in which a physician is held by his fellows, and by the public. And his professional qualifications are a matter of record. It can safely be assumed that any licensed psychiatrist has received the formal education and training that convinced a board of examiners he was competent to practice his profession. Sources of information such as the American Psychiatric Association and the National Committee for Mental Health doubtless can place lists of psychiatrists in a given locality at the disposal of the inquirer. Social agencies are usually in touch with psychiatrists, and one's own physician can usually refer a patient to some good man.

It is hard to tell how good a psychiatrist might be in the case of a given patient. Doctor A may be just the man for Patient X, but he may not be able to reach Patient Y. And Patient X, who swears by Doctor B, might be quite inaccessible to Doctor A. The good psychiatrist, when he sees a patient failing to make a satisfactory response to his efforts after a sufficient length of time has elapsed, is quick to suggest that the patient seek another doctor. And this in part answers the question whether one should change doctors if he feels that he is not being helped.

The questions being considered here are applicable only where men might feel moved to seek help. What about the cases where a criminal court orders a man to undergo psychotheraphy in lieu of serving a prison sentence? Or what about the cases where securing treatment is made part of an order of probation? In many cases such as this, the old saw has a certain validity: "A man convinced against his will remains of the same opinion still." Considerable doubt has been cast upon the usefulness of treatment in cases of this sort. Not a few psychiatrists refuse to treat patients who come to them, lest a worse fate befall them. One or two British physicians of some eminence regard forced treatment as wasteful—to say the least. And they go so far as to say that it is downright immoral to compel a man to try to change his nature. There are those who consider it a violation of our laws for a court to direct what is, in effect, "brain washing." As against that, there is always the hope that a man embarking upon treatment against his desire might, before the journey is over, come to see how he might profit therefrom. This is a neat problem of ethics.

It is axiomatic that the state has the power to coerce the citizen to behave in any way it sees fit, and that it may take any steps it deems desirable to produce that result. But the morality of the transaction is open to a great deal of question. In a police state, the individual is told what to do, and that is the end of the matter. In a democracy, however, the enforcement and administration of the law depend upon the consent of the governed. It is assumed that the effect of a law and the means of enforcing obedience thereunto will have been earnestly considered by the people's representatives in their legislatures before they are adopted.

A person suffering from a communicable disease is taken in hand for treatment, and no one troubles himself to inquire whether his convenience may suffer. Here the public safety is involved. One supposes that a man who is foolish enough to refuse treatment when he hurts his big toe can well be left to his own devices until the pain convinces him to see a doctor. In one case, the presence of a communicable disease calls for drastic action to deal with an impending danger to the body social. It is obvious that a community must protect itself, and, in the process, help the sufferer, with or without his approval.

It is not so clear that the same threat exists in the case of the homosexual. Has society the right to order him to take treatment, whether he will or no? Has he the right to say, "I am aware of the risks entailed in my position, and am prepared to take the consequences?" Does he present so great a social menace that he must be treated against his will because he was unfortunate enough to get arrested? As against this, there is a fairly general feeling that all of us might use with profit a little or a great deal of psychiatry. Many homosexuals have been helped quite materially; even though the occasion of helpfulness involved a bit of coercion in the beginning, when the judge offered the offender the choice between treatment and a prison term.

This conflict could not arise in a dictatorship. There Father Knows Best; his sons, willing or unwilling, march off to the treatment room when they are so ordered. In a democracy it is not as simple as all that. There it is assumed that limitations are placed upon the exercise of power; most democracies do not feel that the end justifies the means. A great deal of thought must be given to the wisdom of compelling men to undergo treatment lest a worse fate befall them. Whether the benefits derived therefrom outweigh what some might think the dubious morality involved in coercion is a matter requiring much thought. All we can do is to suggest the problem.[9]

What happens when a judge places a homosexual on probation who feels that he is right and society is wrong? He has been ordered to take treatment to learn the error of his ways. Sending such a man to be treated for what he considers none of society's business can pose some uncomfortable problems. His situation on probation is even more equivocal. He is put in the position of having to lie to his probation officer about his private life, or openly defying the court. Enforced treatment is a mixed blessing. It can be justified only when the court is persuaded beyond peradventure that the need for homosexuals to conform is the clear and unmistakably expressed will of the people. Today one is not so sure that this is the case.

So long as he manages to avoid arrest or otherwise put himself in a position where he can be ordered to take treatment by the constituted authorities, the homosexual can, under our present system, take treatment or leave it. If he feels strong enough to resist community pressures and is willing to assume what might be called the occupational risks of being a homosexual, then he would do well to remember Somerset Maugham's translation of an old Spanish proverb: "Take what you want out of life; but remember, you have to pay for it."

In other and more direct words, the homosexual who wishes to flit from flower to flower does well to bear in mind some of the disastrous things that lie in wait for him while he busies himself gathering rosebuds. Such a man, when disaster befalls him, is more than a little apt to be forgetful of the long time he was able to avoid paying the bill that might be presented at any hour of the day or night. One practical benefit of consulting a psychiatrist might be to come to some conclusions about the value of hedonism as a way of life. And one might be helped to make some much needed distinctions between lasting and ephemeral values. Many of us are more than a bit hazy about these.

Few homosexuals are what they are because of their own deliberate choosing. At best, they must accommodate themselves to a society conditioned to despise and reject them. It is the rare soul who can go through life untouched by the opinion of a social order that makes him an object of scorn and contumely. It is wisdom of the most earthly sort for the homosexual to seek and utilize help that is designed to rid him of an incubus; or, failing that, to enable him to live with it in more or less comfort. Until society radically changes its views with respect to the sexually maladjusted, he would do well to consider the wisdom of taking advantage of the therapeutic resources that are available.

Ideally, the matter of treatment is one that should be considered by the patient while the decision to take or leave it is his to make. He may come to it with misgivings, as many do; but he must have some feeling that it might better his position. For a long time to come, the homosexual is destined to live in a world that is not disposed to make many allowances for his sexual nonconformity. Despite this forbidding, even hostile, aspect of the external world, psychotherapy has been the means whereby many were enabled to find themselves, and lead useful and richly rewarding lives. Doubtless there are other ways to achieve this result. It is not for us to say that a man rejects treatment at his peril. But surely it would do us no harm to become much better acquainted with ourselves than most of us imagine we are. There is nothing new about this. It is as old as the Greek philosopher's injunction to know ourselves.

CHAPTER V

THE VOICE OF THE LAW

When we speak of law, we ordinarily mean *human* law, the law that regulates the transactions and relations between men in their social life, the law that defines their rights and duties, civil liability and criminal responsibility, and prescribes remedies for wrongs.

—*John H. C. Wu[1]*

The laws of any society must be acceptable to the general moral sense of the community if they are to be accepted and enforced.

——*The Wolfenden Report*

Sir William Blackstone defined law as a rule of conduct coming from the King, commanding what was right and prohibiting what was wrong. In a democratic society, the authority to make laws comes from the people, who empower their chosen representatives to enact the statutes that are necessary for the orderly government of the land. Laws thus made are binding upon all the inhabitants thereof.

Those who fail in obedience must expect to respond in punishment. Penalties for infractions of the laws are determined by the lawmakers' notions of the seriousness of the offenses. Malefactors of former days were killed, whipped, branded, mutilated; they were made slaves or sent to the galleys. Today we put our criminals in prison. The Biblical requirement of an eye for an eye and a tooth for a tooth still influences the making of our legal codes.

Crime was considered an end in itself, to be wiped out by legislation. Men failed to realize, as Dr. Wu points out, that "It does not belong to human law to prescribe all the virtues and repress all the vices. Human law has often been a subject of ridicule to laymen; when they see the law does not prohibit all the vices and prescribe all the virtues, they infer, quite unwarrantably, that law is immoral, or at least amoral. They do not realize that there are limits to effective human action."[2]

Societies still try to make men law-abiding by punishing conduct they deem reprehensible. The threat of dire consequences, both in this world and in the world to come, has thus far had little effect as a salutary means to restrain criminals. The law concerns itself with the preservation of public order as a needful step in the promotion of the common good. "Good morals," as John H. C. Wu sees the process, "constitute an essential ingredient of the common good. In fact, public morals and good order are the twin motors of the legal mechanism."[3]

Anglo-Saxon society undertook to keep the motors in order with respect to sex offenders by seeing to it that they received harsh treatment. Homosexuals fared worse than many others. The voice of the law was clear and unequivocal. At the dawn of the Reformation, it prescribed death in a most unpleasant fashion for those who participated in "the abominable and detestable crime against nature, not to be mentioned among Christians." Prior to that, when the homosexual fell into trouble in the British Isles, the ecclesiastical courts dealt with him. There he was made uncomfortable enough to realize that the Church did not look upon him with any great tolerance; but the punishments meted out by the Spiritual judges fell far short of the savagery that was later to be his lot.

Needless to say, legislation has not wiped out the homosexual offenses, despite the brutal punishments prescribed for those it hoped to make good by an Act of Parliament. For many years the Church had sought to subjugate the flesh. Often it was able to enlist the aid of the State in its enterprises to improve men's morals by coercion.

All of the British commonwealths and American states have laws designed to punish homosexual offenses. These are discussed, with reference to Britain, in Dr. Sherwin Bailey's studies dealing with homosexuals and the law,[4] and the state of affairs in America is dealt with in Judge Morris Ploscowe's Sex and the Law.[5] Up to yesterday, society sought to punish the offense; it succeeded only in punishing the offender. Its philosophy was punitive and retributive. It was the offense with which the law was concerned, and the fact that a human being happened to be the offender made very little difference to the philosophers of punishment. Not too many centuries ago, in the Middle Ages, a pig and a dog were put to death for hersey in France.[6] None the less, we are coming to recognize, albeit very slowly, that offenses against the criminal law are not ends in themselves. There can be no crime without a context; and the context is the whole of human nature and conduct. Wherein are the sexually connected offenses especially reprehensible? Who and what made them so? One way of looking at the matter is that of St. Paul: "Is the law sin? God forbid. Nay, I had not known sin, but by the law: for I had not known lust save the law had said, Thou shalt not covet."[7]

The law seeks to grade crimes according to their seriousness. The legal philosophers distinguished between offenses that were *mala in se*, literally evil in themselves, and those regarded as *mala prohibita*, or acts forbidden by legislative rule. Society deals more severely with crimes that are generally recognized as evil than it does with acts the state deems it necessary to forbid in the common interest. Or so at least the theory runs. By and large, there are less stigma and penalty attached to trying to smuggle a bit of jewelry into the country than there is for housebreaking.

There can be little doubt as to the attitude of the lawmakers with respect to the homosexual offenses, as one examines the language used to define them. The British and American statutes follow the language employed by King Henry the Eighth's Parliament in expressing condemnation of the moral turpitude involved in the acts singled out for punishment. Sodomy is one of the milder epithets employed; and the description of the act as the crime against nature is one of the more mentionable epithets by which the lawbooks describe a crime considered unmentionable. From the way in which the offense is spread out on the statutes, little doubt is left, either in the minds of the offenders or those who hale them to court, how society feels about this variety of sexual experience.

The enforcement of the law against homosexual acts in this country is relatively haphazard. So far as the major offenses are concerned, it would not appear that there is much concerted attempt on the part of the police to ferret out acts of homosexual intercourse committed in private. Save for evil chance, it is doubtful that the circumspect have much to fear from the law-enforcement agencies.

Of course there is always the chance of a disgruntled individual turning on a sexual companion with whom he has fallen out. It is doubtful that the police pay much attention to homosexual lovers' quarrels; nor is it likely that the machinery of the law will be put at the disposal of a discarded sexual companion. Furthermore, both parties being equally guilty under the law, there is some danger involved when one goes to the police to complain about a crime that might also put the informer himself out of circulation.

Homosexual offenses against the young are apt to be prosecuted as charges of impairing the morals of minors. The police do act to break up bawdy parties that disturb the peace. Most of the homosexual offenses in Metropolitan New York that reach the courts arise out of episodes detected in public places—parks and beaches, railway and subway toilet rooms, solicitation on public streets and other gathering places. These usually follow complaints by citizens of molestation or annoyance at the hands of homosexuals who attempt to force their attentions upon those who have no interest in them. For the most part, the police concern is primarily with the preservation of public order; and defendants apprehended in places not intended for the convenience of homosexuals are dealt with as nuisances.

In addition to the legitimate activities of the police, homosexuals would do well to be wary of individuals who profess to be detectives. These men find public parks and comfort stations a lucrative source of blackmail. They permit homosexuals to make advances to them, sometimes encouraging them to commit an unlawful act. Then something that looks like a police badge is shown, and what appears to be the form of an arrest takes place. These pretended policemen can sometimes be bought off with small sums. The amateurs among them prefer to make a single killing, rather than make a rendezvous at which the victim may appear, not only with money but also a lawful officer prepared to arrest an extortionist. However, when a blackmail ring that knows the ropes is in operation, the victim can be bled white. The police are understandably quite anxious to assist men who are courageous enough to come forward and complain against extortionists.

Ordinarily homosexuals who testify against their despoilers can be reasonably sure of protection. However, an unscrupulous attorney for a blackmailer can make the complainant quite uncomfortable on the witness stand. One attorney for a blackmail ring dug up enough information to make one wonder whether the blackmailer or his victim was on trial. When protest was made to the judge that the defense attorney was badgering the complaining witness, the judge ruled that a lawyer had the right to do his best to discredit the prosecution's case, by proving out of the State witness's own lips that he had the sort of character that made his testimony unworthy of belief. The judge said that the District Attorney ought to have warned his witness that he would be subject to this type of inquisition if he took the stand. He realized that it was somewhat unpleasant for the complainant to have details of his private life unearthed that he hoped would not be ventilated in a courtroom; but he could not deprive the defense of the right to make the most of its opportunity to discredit the man who brought charges of a serious nature. Fortunately not all judges allow such a wide latitude in cross examination of complainants in extortion cases.

Consternation is occasionally expressed by homosexuals at what might be called the officious and unwarranted way in which some policemen arrest them. They may accompany the act of arrest with epithets. When, as sometimes is said to be the case, homosexuals complain of being beaten by the arresting officer at the time of their apprehension, this is brushed aside with a story that the man sustained an accident; or, if he shows too many signs of a beating, he is said to have resisted arrest and had to be subdued. The rules permit a policeman to employ only the measure of force required to subdue an individual when he resists arrest. Who is to say what that measure of force shall be? Reports of beatings are heard with sufficient frequency from persons of many walks of life to cause concern about the manner in which homosexuals are treated when they are taken into custody. There seems little doubt that stories of police brutality are not altogether without foundation. Nor can one avoid the observation that the generally held prejudice against homosexuals is reflected in the manner in which some policemen discharge the function of apprehending those who must answer to a court for behavior that is against the law.

A very interesting question is raised by the use of entrapment in connection with arrests in public places. It has been heard many times that a policeman will engage a suspect in conversation, and deliberately lead him on to the place where his conduct warrants an arrest. More infrequently one hears that a policeman has behaved in such manner as to cause a homosexual to feel that he has fallen in with an individual bent on similar purpose. One or two judges have justified entrapment on the ground that there seemed no other way of bringing this type of malefactor to justice. None the less, some doubts remain as to the morality of the transaction—apart from the mountain going into labor and bringing forth a little, ridiculous mouse. Should society allow a zealous policeman even to seem to participate in a transaction it professes to regard with horror? Certainly the psychological effect of seeming participation in such a performance should be taken into account. What happens within the minds of the policemen who are engaged in this type of crime detection day after day? If the law expects them to look at these offenses with the same detachment as burglaries, then, as Mr. Bumble tells us in *Oliver Twist*, "the law is a ass, a idiot." A state professing to have some interest in the moral welfare of its police force should give some thought to what peering through holes in a subway washroom does to those who peer. And certainly considerable thought needs to be given to the moral justification of sending policemen out to tempt homosexuals and prostitutes to commit the acts society professes to abhor.

Of the need for reform there is no doubt. It is a little difficult imagining the Good Society commanding its servants to go out into the highways and hedges to tempt weak men to commit the acts for which it proposes to punish them. Is the law so greatly in need of victims that it must go out of its way to lead the fallible into temptation? What does entrapment prove? That human beings can be enticed into situations not altogether of their own making is something that does not need repeated demonstration.

New light is constantly being thrown on the causes and conditions of crime. And crime includes the sexual offenses. Daily we are learning more about the offenses that have a sexual frame of reference. The workers in the behavioral sciences are accumulating a vast body of knowledge in respect thereto. Unfortunately, although there are some who think it just as well, it generally takes the law a long time to accommodate itself to what is the property of the scientific market place. That is probably in the nature of things. None the less, there is a new view of the criminal law slowly emerging. Sometimes it takes centuries to see changes; once in a while they come with incredible swiftness, when we see a legislature giving heed to a clamant public conscience.

More than a century ago, Chief Justice Taney, in the Dred Scott case, held it to be the law of the land that a Negro had no rights a white man was bound to respect. By extrapolation one can draw a picture of the rights of convicted felons. There is no doubt that, until very recently, both suffered at the hands of those who felt that they could do no special harm to men who were less than men before the law.

Few thought to question the severity of revengeful social punishments. A change is rapidly taking place in our thinking. There is emerging the idea of the law as something more than an instrument of retribution. There was a time when criminal statutes were regarded as the laws of the Medes and the Persians. But statutes were discovered to have outlived their usefulness. We see such a view expressed in one of the edicts of the Emperor Justinian: "To make a law to adjust an evil is like giving medicine. You can't tell what effect it will have ... We have decided it is necessary to change not only the edicts of previous emperors, but even our own ... Because human nature goes her way—it leads us to make new enactments."[8]

Men who have served prison sentences sometimes felt moved to write about their experiences. Some of the accounts were excellent as literature; others ran from mediocrity to sheer trash. Of the men who wrote of their prison lives—some of them rebellious souls—few questioned the justice of the punishment inflicted upon them. They seemed to accept the right of society to make and enforce criminal laws. Although they complained of the stupidity, and even the brutality, of officialdom, at no point did the writers wonder about the right of the State to single out their conduct and punish it. Complaints there were of the length of sentences imposed; but of the right of the community to punish, not a moment's doubt existed in the minds of those who were dealt with in this wise. So, up to now, it is not beyond the bounds of possibility to say that homosexuals themselves acquiesced in the popular feeling about what they did, as this was expressed in the penalties detected men were obliged to suffer. In their case, *Vox populi, vox Dei.* The people's representatives decreed that homosexuals were reprehensible and worthy of punishment. And, so far as can be determined, the convicts who had commerce with the voice of God as it was mediated through prison chaplains, were left with no illusions as to where they stood in the divine scheme of things.

All prisons did was to exacerbate the guilt feelings that homosexuals brought with them to their place of punishment. It is difficult to see how an institution designed to repress can bring about the rehabilitation the more optimistic keepers of such establishments hope to set afoot. For the most part, prisons embitter their inmates; they increase their hostility to the society that sent them there. In *Erewhon,* Samuel Butler suggests a somewhat different approach to the general problem of criminal behavior. He proposes that the sick should be flogged and imprisoned, and the criminals be sent to doctors he called straighteners. We are commencing to see the need for straighteners to help those we adjudged criminals to more adequate ways of life. Hitherto we had dealt with them on the theory that, if we made their lives hard enough, there might be some hope for a reformation. With amazing optimism, we called the place wherein prisoners were kept penitentiaries. For a long time, we have been suspecting that this method of animal taming had its shortcomings. It is a commonplace that the reform school, so called, is a way station to the state prison. All the old-style penal institution did was to separate the detected offender from the rest of society—and that only for a time. The penal system helped create a criminal subsociety, which certainly had little but animosity for the social order that cast its members into outer darkness. Of the efficacy of our methods of dispensing criminal justice, Mr. Justice Holmes asks some inconvenient questions—such as: "What have we better than a blind guess that the criminal law in its present form does more good than harm? I do not stop to refer to the effect it has had in degrading prisoners and plunging them further into crime, or to question whether fine and imprisonment do not fall more heavily on a criminal's wife and children. I have in mind some more far-reaching questions. Does punishment deter? Do we deal with criminals on proper principles?'"

Thus did Judge Holmes apply a pragmatic test to the criminal law. What is accomplished by punishing those who disobey the law's commandments? In particular cases, it might be unwise to permit an individual who repeatedly offends to remain at large. And there is a whole army of misfits whose members return again and again to the prison. Still one wonders with Justice Holmes how much the prison serves any useful purpose in making our social casualties into useful citizens. Centuries of severity, even of brutality, have not accomplished this. Certainly it is a rare homosexual who is helped by serving a term in a penal institution. So far as this phase of our social thinking is concerned, we have much to learn.

The social conscience of the Anglo-Saxon world is commencing to show signs of uneasiness because of treatment of sexual nonconformists as criminals. In England a proposal was placed before the House of Commons to remove the private sexual intercourse of two consenting adults of full age from the list of punishable offenses. And in this country, the model criminal code put forth by the American Law Institute takes adultery and the private homosexual intercourse of adults out of the jurisdiction of the criminal courts.

Thus far society has considered the homosexual a serious threat to its security. In few other types of criminal prosecution do as many frankly punitive elements appear as in the cases of men charged with homosexual crimes. Hitherto the homosexual has been made to feel his position most acutely. He is never permitted to forget the contemptuous manner in which society permits the police and minor court officials to treat him. A graduate student in a university in metropolitan New York—ordinarily a fairly level-headed individual—describes his court appearance and what preceded it as a nightmare. This man was not particularly conspicuous in appearance, dress or behavior; he bore none of the distinguishing marks that the popular imagination ascribes to all homosexuals. He had been held overnight to await his preliminary hearing and have bail fixed. He says that, when he was arrested, the policeman who took him into custody called him all the vile names he could think up. When, dishevelled and sleepless, he appeared before the magistrate the next morning, he felt that the cold, impersonal recitation of the details of his offense and the questions about how he proposed to plead were so mechanical that he might have been hearing voices coming out of a phonograph. Assuming that the State has a right, and perhaps even a duty, to proscribe and penalize conduct it deems contrary to its well-being, there still remains a corresponding duty for the citizen from time to time to call into question the methods employed by its servants to secure obedience to the social laws. In the conservative language of the Wolfenden Report: "Not all the elements in the apprehension of offenders, or in their trial, seem to us to be satisfactory."[10]

Here it might be well to pause to see, if we can, why the law and its officers take so strongly punitive a view of the homosexual and his legal offenses. Wherein does he present such a serious threat to the security of society? Again the Wolfenden Report sheds some useful light:

"In considering whether homosexual acts between consenting adults ... should cease to be criminal offenses, we have examined the more serious arguments in favour of retaining them as such ... In favour of retaining the present law, it has been contended that homosexual behaviour between adult males, in private no less than in public, is contrary to the public good on the grounds that— (1) it menaces the health of society; (2) it has damaging effects on private life; (3) a man who indulges in these practices with another man may turn his attention to boys." [11]

The Wolfenden Committee considers such reasoning specious and fallacious. But legislators have made their chief concern the discovery of evil to be punished. They were persuaded that it is the function of the social order to "command what is right and prohibit what is wrong."[12] In order to bring this about, punishment is to be expected to be the inevitable consequence of behavior made criminal by legislative enactment. This is the sort of philosophy that helped to form the thinking of the framers of the criminal law. They seemed more concerned with "the punishment of wickedness and vice" than for the "maintenance of true religion and virtue."[13] Nor does there seem to be any reason to believe that our ancestors were convinced of the triumph of goodness in their time. They did not regard its opposite with too much horror; they seemed resigned to the universality and ineradicability of sin. Especially were they convinced of the likelihood of having to contend for a long time with the sins of the flesh. And their gloomiest view was reserved for those whose carnal derelictions took the form of homosexual acts. For them they reserved

their choicer anathemas. There may be some improvement in today's view of the state of the sexual deviator. If there is, the improvement is almost imperceptible.

In dealing with its criminals with a heavy hand, the community
shows its fear of the threat they might present. It undertook to fight
fire with fire when it wrote its condemnation of their conduct into its
penal laws. There are judges who like to hear themselves called the
terror of evildoers. It is doubtful that the power they possess to
inflict punishment strikes as much fear in the heart of a criminal about
to be sent to prison as what has been going on in the most seemingly
hardened convict's mind. Bravado and hostility are well used masks
to cover fear and shame and guilt.

This is not new. For a long time, there has been a growing feeling
that severity of punishment failed to repress crime or do very much
to protect society. Much less did it fail to dissuade criminals from
committing their offenses. In recent years, significant reductions have
been made in the length of sentences authorized by law, and the public
slowly commences to take cognizance of the fact that criminals, as one
penologist put it, are people.

Within a somewhat less degree, the notion has begun to have some
applicability to homosexuals. The new science of penology, the results
of the investigations of the psychiatrists and the psychologists, and, to
a very limited degree, the acceptance of the doctrine of the evolution-
ary nature of our ethical ideas, have all had a share in the production
of newer attitudes toward crime and punishment. Because so much
emotion is involved in the sexual offenses, especially the homosexual
ones, society has been much slower to relinquish the fears for its
security posed by those involved in sexual conduct deemed abnormal
and criminal. That is one of the reasons why homosexuals fare so
badly in the criminal courts.

Basically, the rigidity of our legislation with respect to prohibited
sexual acts reflects the desire of the community to enforce what it
considers proper standards of morality. The wisdom of this has been
questioned by Woodrow Wilson: "Morality is a great deal bigger than
law. The individual morality is the sense of right or wrong of one
man. The social morality must strike an average. That is where
the reformers make their tragic mistake. There can be no compromise
with individual morality, but there has to be an average, a compromise,
in social morality. There is indeed an element of morality in the very
fact of compromise in social undertakings."[4]

The scientific approach to the problem of delinquency in general has had its repercussions in the realm of sex offenses. Even though harsh laws remain on the statute books, there is hope of a more realistic attitude spreading downward and outward. It is still decidedly impossible for the man in the street, so-called, to view the homosexual offender with the same charity that he can contemplate a housebreaker.

New light is constantly being thrown on the causes and conditions of crime—and crime includes sexual offenses. The psychiatric literature, for instance, is enormous. The contributions of psychiatry toward the understanding of the homosexual are commencing to affect the operations of the criminal courts. Jurisprudence has taken cognizance of what is being done in the social and psychological sciences, and what is called sociological jurisprudence is the subject of at least lip service by those who tend the machines that grind out the processes of the criminal law. The effect of the newer scientific thinking is considered by Mr. Justice Frankfurter in this wise:

"We still do not know what is chargeable to nature and irremediable by men. Nor do we know to what extent what is good in nature is thwarted by man's institutions—what potentialities can be realized that are now frustrated. One may well assume that the biological factors are important in the maladjustments that beget crime. But awareness of the truth hardly tells us what are the biological factors, their extent and their significance.

"We have lived to see biological fictions and fantasies employed as justification for the most brutal practices. That has made us more wary than ever of untested biological explanations. On the other hand ... criminal acts are apt to be the product of the interplay of complex pressures and resistances that are but ill described and dealt with as though they constituted a single dominating spring of action called criminal intent.

"Doctrines and judgements are no stronger than the facts on which they are based ... The characteristic of law in a progressive society is an adjustment between continuity and change. Our criminal codes should not too rapidly accommodate themselves to the latest guidance of scientific inquiry. But it is equally fatal to be heedless of such guidance. Whatever our metaphysical notions about the freedom of the will may be, we can no longer rest content with the conception of criminal intent as an expression of full free choice between doing a proscribed act and not doing it. Again, the inadequacy of our traditional methods for determining the appropriate treatment for offenders, once wrongdoing is established, can no longer be disregarded ...

"Social phenomena like crime are imbedded in the texture of our society. To be understood they cannot be severed from the total environment. Only complacency will assume that the maladjustments which underlie crime are all reflected in our criminal statistics. And so, just as the study of disease illumines pathological processes that are not pathological, critical and persistent inquiry into the social pathology that is crime ought greatly to further understanding of the interplay between society and the individual in its many manifestations that happily are not the concern of the criminal courts."[15]

In effect, the criminal law seeks to separate the sheep from the goats. It establishes a complicated machinery to discover wrongdoers and bring them to justice. Then, employing a complicated hierarchy, with a multitude of rules for the guidance of its priests, levites and acolytes, it separates the good from the bad. It consigns those it accounts criminal to the outer darkness of the prison cell or the death chamber, and it is careful to commend to the mercy of the Almighty the souls of those whom the sentence of the law condemns to death.

Nor does society's demand for its pound of flesh end when the prison doors open to discharge the offender whose term has expired. Those who read in Chapter II of what happened to a literate young man who was imprisoned for a homosexual offense will recall that his punishment continued long after the expiration of his prison sentence. He had to take work paying much less money than what he earned at the time of his arrest. The consideration of giving him a job permitting him to leave prison was shown him because a socially minded citizen was unsure that justice had been done. So great was the public hostility to a known homosexual who had served a prison sentence that he was obliged to move to a great city, where he might live unnoticed. Only thus could he hope to take up the threads of his interrupted career. Fortunately this man had enough force of character to make a place for himself in a new environment. He still lives in some fear, lest he betray himself. He enjoys the good luck of having an employer who knows about his time of trouble, and who will protect him against the possibility of a blackmailer threatening to expose him at his place of work. This man had good fortune. What of the men without friends powerful enough to help them find suitable work and a chance for the restoration of the self-respect that prison may have destroyed?

The punishment of the law can go far beyond the service of a prison sentence. There may be those who wonder why criminals go through what Austin MacCormick called the revolving doors of the prison.

Why, some may ask, do they lack character enough to straighten themselves out? It is doubtful that those who ask questions of this sort are very perceptive. Certainly they cannot have much acquaintance with the roots of crime, or the compulsions that drive so many men to desire to encompass their own destruction. If this be true of the maladjustments called criminal behavior in general, how much more true is this of the homosexual who falls foul of the law and lives with the feeling that the finger of social scorn is constantly being pointed at him?

What can society hope to accomplish by the imprisonment of homosexuals? Certainly it is not fatuous enough to consider that imprisonment will reform him or even terrify him into conformity. All a punitive law can do is frighten the man into desisting from overt homosexual activity—thus, perhaps, giving him a somewhat more acceptable neurosis—make him a little more cautious in avoiding not the occasion of sin, but the occasion of being taken in sin.

Too many convicts emerge from prison embittered men. In some cases, their resentments and hostilities, as has been suggested, make them enemies of society and a real threat to the security of the community. It is the exceptional prisoner who feels impelled to kiss the rod and thank the court for sending him to a penal establishment. How much more embittered, then, is the homosexual who goes to prison in the knowledge that many wiser than he have grave doubts whether the offense that cost him his liberty should be included in the list of punishable crimes.

Here is the anomaly of our laws. So far as one can determine, it is not a crime to be a homosexual. Dr. Bailey calls it a morally neutral state. To commit an act of homosexual intercourse is a crime, punishable by a prison term that could last for the duration of a man's natural life. It becomes abundantly clear that the law in relation to homosexual acts is in need of a great deal of thoughtful reconsideration.

There was a time when the treatment of the insane included imprisonment, the use of chains, flogging, and all manner of cruelty. Perhaps those who devised this method of treating sick people thought that suffering was good for souls in torment. Occasionally, one supposes, a patient survived. There was a time, not too long ago, when the keepers of prisons and lunatic asylums made a good thing of charging the public for the privilege of witnessing the sufferings of the convicts and the demented; and, for a fee, the spectators were permitted to gratify their own sadism by doing a little tormenting of the chained convicts or lunatics. There are still prisons and mental hospitals that tolerate the cruel treatment of those committed to their charge. Our progress in the care of those for whom the social order should have a special concern is not an even thing. And, when it comes to the homosexual, Dr. Bailey does well to suggest that the society that will give the penitent thief a chance still finds it necessary to ventilate its hostility on the homosexual.

The law sends men to prison for committing homosexual offenses. If, as was suggested in an earlier chapter, they find opportunity while there to do that for which they were imprisoned in the first place, so far, as the law is concerned, that is a *non sequitur*. Prisons do burn a pinch of incense at the altar of trying to stamp out homosexuality among the population. However, much mcre surveillance than the limitations of staff permits, would be required to control the sexual activities of dwellers in such places. Attempts at segregation succeed only in isolating those known to the administration as homosexual. Practically speaking, those who are supposed to know say that more activity goes on between inmates in the general population than takes place in the segregated quarters of all save the most efficiently invigilated prisons. Those who hope to eliminate the Old Adam of sexual desire by locking men into cells are, to put it mildly, optimistic.

Prisons exist to restrain those who violate the law Here, then, our concern should be with what the law seeks to accomplish by imprisonment of homosexuals. In the words of the Wolfenden Report:

"It is not the function of the law to intervene in the private lives of citizens, or to seek any particular pattern of behaviour ... Its function, as we see it, is to preserve public order and decency, to protect the citizen from what is offensive or injurious, and to provide sufficient safeguards against exploitation and corruption of others, especially those who are vulnerable because they are young, weak in body or mind, or in a state of special physical, official or economic dependence.

"It follows that we do not believe it to be a function of the law to attempt to cover all the fields of sexual behavior. Certain forms of sexual behaviour are regarded by many as sinful, morally wrong or objectionable for reasons of conscience, or of religious or cultural tradition. But the criminal law does not cover all such action at the present time; for instance adultery and fornication are offences for which a person can be punished by the criminal law ...

"We clearly recognize that the laws of any society must be acceptable to the general moral sense of the community if they are to be respected and enforced. But we are not charged to enter into matters of private moral conduct except in so far as they affect the public good; nor does our commission extend to assessing the teaching of theology, sociology or psychology on these matters, although on many points we have found their conclusions very relevant to our thinking."[116]

It is the law's business to fix limits of conduct that the community can tolerate. Through imprisonment, the State gives evidence of its disapproval of what, unchecked, may present a threat to its security. At one time the community may have acquiesced in the imposition of the severest sort of penalties for homosexual offenses, as doubtless it approved cruel punishments for all manner of crime. But, through the ages, it has come to take another view of the efficacy of punishment as a means to counteract behavior that fails to meet its approval. Responsible voices have been raised to demand that the social order employ other means than repression to regulate the behavior it finds offensive. The Wolfenden Report has, on the whole, met with favorable public response. Doubtless the forces of conservatism will, for a time, be able to prevent its recommendations from becoming law. These forces can always be counted upon to delay social change as long as possible. Sooner or later, the recommendations will find their way to the statute books. And, quite a bit later, we may expect to see something of the same sort in this country. In many respects we are a great deal more resistant of schemes that involve social change than the British.

The Wolfenden Report advocates nothing new or startling. It legalizes what society tacitly tolerates, save at those times and seasons when zealots with nothing better to do can harry the police into starting a vice crusade. It is doubtful that the police, if left alone, trouble themselves overmuch about what is done by adults behind closed doors. The State of New York had, and may still have, a statute on its books that would put an adulterer in prison. All a district attorney looking for business need do would be to collect names and addresses from the registers of the divorce courts. Adultery is the only ground for divorce in New York. How many adulteries reach the Grand Jury?

The majority of the Wolfenden Committee evidently felt that the consenting homosexual intercourse of two adults was a private matter, and, as such, of no concern to the Public Prosecutor. Such conduct could conceivably be offensive to many members of the public, and it could easily be what the churches consider sin. As such, it must be left to be dealt with by the clergy who have their own methods of helpfulness to sinners. There are those to whom the notion of sin is unacceptable. They must deal with the problems of their moral imperfections in the forum of conscience. All of us, sooner or later, have to come to terms with our ethical concepts. Doubtless the signers of the Wolfenden Report felt that those who chose to become involved in homosexual episodes with other adults of sufficient age were best left to decide for themselves how what took place affected their moral lives. What took place between the two men was confined, in its effects, to the participants.

For an act to be a crime, its effect must extend beyond its participants. In Dr. Wu's words, it must contravene public order. There was a time when a homosexual episode was thought to do just that. No one had much doubt that it violated the public decencies. Today another view is possible.

Slowly the state, in its social laws, is trying to distinguish between matters of private morality and acts detrimental to the public sense of acceptable conduct on the part of the citizen. It has relinquished control over many aspects of the private lives of men and women that were long considered to be of general concern. And today the State seems moving in several directions ruthlessly to invade its members' rights to privacy. Times change. Once heresy was considered a grave public wrong; it affronted the people's sense of religious unity. Today we feel that heretics may safely be left to their own devices. They are seen to present no threat to the security of the commonwealth. Communists may still preach their gospel freely, so long as they refrain from overt acts that might endanger the state. It is not inconceivable that the time may come when they will impress the guardians of our liberties as a source of real or potential danger. Then further curbs may be expected to limit their freedom quite seriously. Thus it was, let us say, with Germans and Japanese during the Second World War.

There was a time when the whole body social considered the homosexual a grave menace. Probably even his worst enemies take a less rigorous view today. To the police he is a nuisance; to those who look upon him with unfriendly eyes, he is something to be avoided; to those of another turn of mind, he is someone who happens to think and act differently about some relatively unimportant matters. Unfortunately we try to enforce today, not too successfully, laws in respect to homosexuals designed to meet yesterday's need. The laws reflects an evolving social conscience. Like King Charles II, who said he took an unconscionable time dying, the law seems to take an unconscionable time catching up with today's social demands.

Chapter VI

THE CHURCH AND THE HOMOSEXUAL:
A RESPONSIBILITY AND AN OPPORTUNITY

Then the Lord said to Cain, "Where is Abel, your brother?" He said, "I do not know. Am I my brother's keeper?"

—*Genesis*[1]

When Adam and Eve were driven from the Garden of Eden, they settled down to make the most of things. In the course of time, they had two sons. Cain, the elder, was a husbandman; Abel, the younger, a shepherd. Abel found favor in the eyes of God and of his parents; and Cain, like many another older brother, failed to understand why the younger boy should be preferred to him. Somewhere along the way, the failure to understand was turned into hatred; and the hatred became so consuming that Cain slew his brother. Murder had been done; and, in this primitive story of the beginning of things, we see the Lord conducting the investigation into the homicide. One of the first things men had to learn was a sense of responsibility. We can see Cain trying to escape the Lord's searching questions: "Where is Abel? What have you done with him?" And we can see Cain trying to escape from his responsibility by answering one question with another: "Am I my brother's keeper?"

Ever since then, men have tried their best to turn a blind eye to what is involved in being their brothers' keepers. It is easy to shrug off a duty by saying, "What business is it of mine?" Or we can try to evade it by professing our insignificance. This attitude has made its way into current American slang: "You can't fight City Hall." When the monks of the West found the corruption of the Roman Empire too much for their efforts, they fled into the desert to avoid contamination. Yet they found the world unwilling to let them stay apart altogether. Sooner or later, men knocked at the monastery doors, demanding that the brethren assume responsibility for more than the care of their own souls.

It is quite easy for the church to look upon the homosexual as an object of scorn and loathing, adopting the attitude of the world that he is to be despised and rejected. Those who need to justify that opinion with support to be derived from ecclesiastical authority have many theologians of untarnished reputation upon whom they can rely.

In the past the church has legislated against the sexual deviate with as much feeling as the State, and it at least made no particular objection to the savage punishments society meted out to those found guilty of intimacies with their own sex. Students who are interested in learning how the church came to the position it did in regard to the problem of homosexuality have a wealth of material available for consultation.

In the past, the church made its attitude toward homosexuality so clearcut and unequivocal that men feared to resort to its ministers in their time of trouble. For the most part, the church's distaste for the problem was so obvious that homosexuals preferred to go without benefit of clergy. They felt that the church regarded them as heretics or worse—quite beyond the charity of Christians.

In its view of the sexual deviate, the church assumed that he was a free agent, capable of his own volition to sin or refrain from sinning. If he found himself in an unenviable position, he had only himself to blame. He put himself there through his own perversity. Thus the institution felt that it could afford to disclaim any sort of responsibility for him. It said in effect that homosexuals excommunicated themselves by their conduct, thus cutting themselves off from fellowship with the faithful. This is why some homosexuals seem to regard themselves beyond redemption. Somewhere they had to be taught how to think in that fashion. Even if it is suggested that this feeling comes from an exaggerated sense of guilt on the part of a distorted personality, it must be remembered that guilt and sin are social concepts. To be effective, opinions as to what constitutes sin must necessarily be widely held. What is the responsibility of the church for those it has permitted to feel that their sins have cut them off from the life and work of the institution that calls itself the Body of Christ?

The function of the church, in the moral realm, is to make bad men good and good men better. Slowly, spurred on by efforts of a forward-looking body within the Church of England, its Moral Welfare Council, it is coming to reconsider its attitudes toward those who feel that they are objects of ecclesiastical *apartheid laws*. Hitherto church and world united to cast the homosexual into outer darkness. It felt its responsibility ended when it had given its judgment. A bishop, when he pronounced sentence of deposition upon a homosexual priest, told him that he was not fit to walk on the same side of the street with decent people. Judgment is not enough. Has this bishop expressed the mind of the whole church in feeling it has discharged its responsibility by getting rid of what it considered an unprofitable servant? If the whole duty of the church toward the homosexuals within it ends with their extrusion, then its duty is very easily done.

Complaint is sometimes levelled against the homosexual that he is irresponsible. Before we pass a blanket judgment on his failures on that score, ought not the church inquire of itself what it had a right to expect from men it casts out when their problems obtruded themselves on the notice of its leaders? And, assuming that there might be something to the indictment, what part have the church and society played in making the homosexual what he is? This question is one that can be asked with equal pertinence of those who complain that members of radical and ethnic groups whom they happen to dislike display undesirable characteristics.

Here is how Father Myers saw the problem as it affected young people whose lives were circumscribed by racial prejudice, poverty, sickness and crime in a depressed area in New York City: "Surely no man can be expected to take his place of responsibility among the brethren if only the way of judgment is used. Nor can he learn of the love of God in his real life situation unless he has experienced, somehow and somewhere, the love of man. And not to know the love of man is the condition of thousands who pass along the city streets." [1]

To re-examine its attitudes in the light of the contributions of the behavioral sciences, and possibly come to different conclusions with respect to the homosexual, will not be easy for the church to do. Sheer inertia, the willingness to let well enough alone and Scriptural fulminations against unhallowed sexual practices, warrant many of the clergy who stop learning the day they leave the divinity school to refuse to reconsider what they think they were taught. This is an understandable human trait not peculiar to the cloth. They had been conditioned to think that men who derived their sexual satisfactions from other men were in parlous, if not hopeless, state. And condemnation is always the line of least resistance.

It takes a great deal of courage to question opinion, especially ecclesiastical opinion. But those in the church who speak to the condition of the homosexual do not ask that his conduct be condoned: all they ask is that the men so conditioned be treated as any other human beings who fall short of its counsels of perfection. It is platitudinous that "while the lamp holds out to burn, the vilest sinner may return." In the thought of too many people, it is highly questionable that the charity of the church can be extended to permit the return of the homosexual, even though he come wearing sackcloth and ashes.

Men are apt to confuse terms with facts. To the unthinking, the term *homosexual* is a red rag waved before a bull. In the minds of such, a vision is conjured up of a somewhat unpleasant, effeminate little man, to whom the epithet *pervert* or *degenerate* can be applied. Or else they think of him as an obnoxious individual, constantly on the prowl for new sexual conquests, and always ready to corrupt the young. To think of a homosexual as one with a concern for another human being, apart from his availability as a sex object, is something quite beyond them. The usual notion of homosexual irresponsibility precludes the possibility that men so characterized can and do feel genuine concern for their fellow men, and are able to translate that concern into useful and acceptable social action. None the less, day after day, homosexuals give devoted service to causes that those who deride him feel far beyond the scope of his interests. Let us look at one homosexual's attempt to discover his duty to his neighbor and take steps to perform it.

Not too long ago, a letter was received from a young man who wrote to the George W. Henry Foundation from a distant city, asking for advice and help. Many years ago, he had been involved in an unpleasant transaction. He had been sent to the Foundation by the Probation Department of a criminal court. The crime that necessitated his being placed on probation consisted of obtaining money under false pretenses. He was required to make restitution of the money he had obtained, and to seek help to come to better terms with himself and the social order. Of his homosexuality there was not a moment's doubt. Nor was there doubt of his promiscuity and blithe irresponsibility. The boy was bright enough, and he had little trouble finding work. But keeping a job was another matter. The Foundation helped him to obtain a position that fortunately was to his liking. And, on the job he was well liked—almost too well liked. He made friends easily—almost too easily. He was always willing to do anything to make himself popular. When he was told that he put forth efforts to buy friendship, he was shocked. As a matter of fact, it was because of this tendency that he became involved in the criminal enterprise that brought him before the court. He was too willing to listen to the importunities of evil companions, stealing to gain the approval of thieves. There was very little in the way of cash that he derived from his participation in the crime. To use a homely expression, he was a weak sister—withal a not unattractive one.

Basically, however, the boy had some good instincts. Although he was painfully aware of what he was doing when he passed worthless checks, he knew the difference between right and wrong. Use was made of the weakness that made him the willing tool of men prepared to influence him for evil to divert his activities toward the opposite direction. Here his pliability was of advantage to those the court appointed to help him. Under probationary supervision the boy —let's call him Jack—gave no trouble. He reported faithfully, was able to reimburse the loser of the stolen money, did well at work, and even got one or two salary increases. In a word, the Probation Department was able to mark his record, when the time came for the period of supervision to be terminated, "Discharged with Improvement."

When he left the jurisdiction of the court, he decided to return to his home, several hundred miles away from New York. He thought—wisely, it subsequently developed—that he would do best in a place where he had roots—family and friends. This he did and there he prospered. His habits of industry, acquired while on probation, stood him in good stead. He got himself an excellent job and held on to it; in it he worked himself up to a responsible and well-paying situation.

His letter was a plea for help with a very serious ethical problem. Although Jack was a fairly regular attendant of a small church in his home community, he preferred, knowing something about small-town gossip, not to put himself in a position, where, with the best will in the world, a part of his life he felt not to be his neighbors' business might become known. So he wrote to the place where he was sure, through the Foundation's church connections, he would get the sort of advice that would be realistic and still take into account the Christian ideals to which he was attached.

Jack and a fellow worker at the plant where both were employed had become friendly. Both young men seemed to have many interests in common; they enjoyed the same social opportunities, and went together occasionally to a nearby city when they had a little money that could be squandered on harmless frivolities. They talked about joining forces and sharing an apartment. For over a year all went well.

As Jack grew in maturity and a sense of responsibility, he felt a very real concern for his friend—let us call him George. George had become dissatisfied with the simple attractions of life in a small town. He showed signs, as Chief Justice Stone put it, of wanting to go to hell in a buggy. He took to drink; he formed undesirable acquaintances; he seemed to be drifting away from his old friends. He associated with persons and frequented places that were much less than wholesome. Worse than that, his work suffered.

So much did George's work suffer that the management, knowing of Jack's friendship for him, asked that he make it clear to his friend that, unless George showed an improvement in a very short time, he would be without a job. The plant superintendent suggested that Jack try to make his friend "get wise to himself," and Jack asked for help to sort out the complicating factors that made what needed to be done to carry out his concern for George a very real problem.

Because Jack had been under the necessity of working out some sort of practical solution of his sexual problems, he had done quite a bit of reading in that field. While in New York he consulted all the literature that was put at his disposal, had attended several lectures, and, considering his youth and educational deficiencies, he had a reasonably adequate stock of knowledge of the subject at his command. In his letter, he wondered if his friend, consciously or unconsciously, was pursuing a course that would lead to disaster. Did he want to be punished for homosexual drives of which he may not even have been fully aware? Lacking the courage to admit this, even to himself, was he behaving in a manner that was certain to bring ruin on himself? In other words, Jack suggested that George could accept punishment for being a drunkard and a spendthrift; but that only so far as outward appearances were concerned. Underneath he wanted to be punished for a latent homosexuality. What there actually was to all this speculation never came to light.

It is certain that Jack wanted to stave off the ruin that seemed inevitable for his friend. He felt that somehow he was responsible for George's plight. How was he to act as his brother's keeper? Should he confront his friend with a catalogue of the things that had gone wrong, and suggest that steps had to be taken to correct them? Should he try to persuade George to get professional help? Or must he simply accept the fact that he was powerless? In other words, Jack's letter, simply put, asks: "What is my moral responsibility?" There is more than a suggestion that Jack wanted to assume some, if not all, of the blame for George's downfall. Clearly he was at his wits' ends. What was he to do?

Jack's dilemma was new to him; but it is old as the time when man first recognized his obligation to help a weaker neighbor. Then there was another aspect to the matter. Jack called attention to the fact that he was far from perfect: he had been a thief; he had been a homosexual and was still one. How much of his concern, he asks, is to be charged to a sexual interest in his friend, even though he had never approached him or, so far as he knew, gave George any clue to the possibility of his being interested in that way? He asks if he is morally fit to help his friend. To that the answer is quick and easy. If we waited to be assured of our moral fitness to give a cup of cold water to a thirsty man, there would be few who dared to act on a generous impulse. Goodness flourishes in unexpected places. Consider the proverbial generosity of the prostitute!

What should be the reply of the church to Jack's appeal for advice? It would be quite easy to say that, unless he changed his mode of living, he could hardly be expected to give disinterested advice; he would do better to keep silence, lest he do more harm than good. There are some moralists who would say that the quicker these two young men parted company the better for all concerned. Nor would it be impossible to find some psychologists who would say that Jack was helping indirectly to contribute to George's downfall, either to put both on a moral level, or that Jack could take some pride in helping to raise a fallen sinner. But that type of thinking fails to take into account the fact that the church is not without its supply of sinners.

The only material available from which to make saints is the sinner. Certainly only the most rigid moral theologian would deny Jack the opportunity for helpfulness. The difficulties come when we sit down to consider the practical ways in which help is to be applied.

This book does not profess to supply the answer to the questions, the searching questions, that Jack put to the Foundation. Nor is it particularly pertinent to supply the very tentative suggestions that were sent in reply. The questions were set down to begin a discussion; we do not presume to supply answers that are generally informative. These must come from the moral theologian and perhaps the psychiatrist who is at home within the framework of the church's ethical positions. This much is certain, and Jack's letter brings it out in the open. There is a very real need to resolve a serious moral conflict to which the church has hitherto been singularly obtuse. It has confined its interest in the homosexual to turning a deaf ear when he knocked at its door. Jack has accepted his responsibility to be his brother's keeper. What advice has the church to give him as to how this is done?

Here one must pose a fundamental question. Is the church willing to accept responsibility for being its homosexual brother's keeper? And on what terms? It has been suggested that there are those within the church who consider its duty done when it escorts the homosexual to the gate and tells him there is no room for him at its inn. And might there not be some theologians who would say that assuredly the church manifests an interest in all men everywhere, but the problem of the homosexual is not so exigent, after all. His problem has waited for a long time: are there not more urgent matters to exercise the church's interest? What, for instance, about the discouraging world outlook? What about the armaments race, and the feeling of impending doom as we search hither and yon for the things that make for peace? What about the implications of putting man-made satellites in the sky? What about the inflation? What about the ever-pressing problems of corruption in business, in government, in radio and television, in the trade unions, and even in college basketball? What about the problems of minorities, such as those of the Negro in the South and in South Africa? Are not all of these more pressing than the ones that concern the homosexual? Is it not important for the church to busy itself about the young who seem destined for delinquent careers? Why should there be so much excitement over what one psychiatrist called a choice collection of pleasure-loving psychopaths?

All of the problems that have been mentioned, and a host of others, too, must find places for themselves on the church's agenda papers. Whether they have precedence over the problem of homosexuality is another matter. It seems to be the generally accepted opinion that God concerns Himself with the welfare of all men everywhere. No matter how it is done, He busies himself as much with the need of the humblest slum dweller as that of the nation with a budget of billions of dollars. The community that dares to speak in His name, the community that calls itself the Divine Society, cannot do otherwise. This is how the church and democratic societies are distinguished from those without interest in what becomes of the individual, and think only in terms of power. There are groups that concern themselves with cruelty to animals: who shall say that their concern is unimportant? There are groups devoted to the preservation of exotic flora and fauna: who shall say that their objects are the aberrations of lunatics? What might be of great moment to one set of human beings can seem quite trival, or even meaningless, to others.

It seems axiomatic that the church has taken upon itself a measure of responsibility for those whose lives it touches. Furthermore its Founder commanded His disciples to carry the Gospel message to the uttermost parts of the earth. The church is not without acquaintance with homosexuals. Where they fit, or even if they fit, into its scheme of things is another matter. Here we would do well to consider some advice from a scholar who is considering another aspect of the problem of how the to deal with the multiplicity of interests that clamor for our attention. It comes from the pen of the anthropologist Margaret Mead, a scientist whose friendship for the Christian way of life is undoubted:

"We live in an age when every inquiry must be judged in terms of urgency. Are such questions about the roles and the possible roles of the sexes academic, peripheral to the central problems of our times? Are such discussions querulous fiddling while Rome burns? I think they are not. Upon the growing accuracy with which we are able to judge our limitations and potentialities, as human beings and in particular as scientists, will depend the survival of our civilization, which we now have the means to destroy. Never before in history has mankind had such momentous choices placed in its hands... The decisions we make now, as human beings who are members of groups with power to act, may bind the future as no man's decisions have ever bound it before ... So, as we stand at the moment in history while we still have choice, when we are just beginning to explore the properties of human relationships as the natural sciences have explored the properties of matter, it is of the very greatest importance which questions we ask, because by the questions we ask we set the answers that we will arrive at, and define the paths along which future generations will be able to advance." [2]

It would not be at all difficult for the church to continue in its disclaimer of responsibility for the homosexual, and support it with a great weight of authority. It would be possible, for instance, to say that it is his conduct that cuts him off from commerce with the faithful. St. Paul admonishes us to be not unequally yoked with unbelievers. Likewise the church has a long history of casting out those who had other views than the prevailing one in its numberless controversies. It is easy for the church to rid itself of those who fail to conform, in one aspect or another, to the standards of thought or conduct it deems minimal for one to hold and still keep the faith, as its official teachers promulgate it. There is always the chance, however, that by so doing the institution could impoverish itself. No one denies the right of those who compose its government to set the standards that regulate eligibility for membership. But one can also wonder whether the application of a little charity to those whose conduct fails to measure up to the standards will not better serve its purpose. Not infrequently has the church has occasion to repent its haste in ridding itself of a heretic. Once in a while the orthodox found themselves a bit poorer when they cast out a holder of unpalatable opinions whom later generations canonized.

New light is constantly being thrown on the sexual behavior of human beings. We are beginning to realize that the sexually deviated are not altogether responsible for the ways in which they derive libidinous gratification. We have just begun to make use of the findings of the social and psychological scientists regarding the sexual side of human nature and conduct. The criminal law has begun to take cognizance of the fact that, behind the acts considered anti-social, there is an interplay of forces that makes a criminal act far less an end in itself than a link in a chain of personality distortion. Governments have not yet been able to punish a crime; all they can do is to penalize those who commit offenses against their laws. And the social order is slowly learning what underlies these offenses of its sick and criminal members. It pays at least lip service to the possibilities of rehabiliation through probation and parole services. Even in the prisons some attempts at reclamation are being made. It is only yesterday, as those things seem to go, that society had begun to question its wisdom in cutting off the criminal as unfit for membership therein. There are still laws on the statute books that deprive a convicted man of his citizenship; but happily ways are being found whereby men who have "paid their debt to society" can be restored to full membership in the body social.

There is a certain similarity between the way the State treats its criminals and the church treats its homosexuals. Both are cut off from citizenship. But the state is slowly re-examining its positions in this matter. The church would do well to follow its example, for the way of understanding is a much more excellent one than the way of judgment. There are still those both in church and state who would confine their interest to the elect. Dr. Mead speaks to the limitations of their charity when she says:

"Pictures of a world in which the clergy could say wholeheartedly, 'We are not interested in civilization; we are interested in colonizing Heaven' may arouse a piercing nostalgia in all who love the Cathedral of Chartres, but by so doing they simply unman one more needed worker in the workshop of civilization. Those who give themselves so wholeheartedly to the lovely and gracious task of colonizing Heaven that they have no time for public health regulations and building codes, by so doing cut themselves off from almost the whole band of colonists whom they would wish to lead gently into the eternal daylight of God's presence. Man's fitness for Heaven, which is perhaps one of the best ways we have thought of to describe man's potentialities that he does *not* share with any other known mammal, is no simple formula that will make modern men and women turn away from the dutiful attention to newly discovered ways of increasing man's fitness on earth. But we need not accept any such dichotomy between earth and Heaven, between bodily needs and spiritual capacities, between limitations and potentialities." [8]

Doubtless what the church in the past held before the faithful as an ideal of moral and theological excellence was useful as a counsel of perfection. But perfection is something that is given to few of us to attain here on earth. The church has yet to realize that those who fall short of its demands on fallible human beings do not set out deliberately to act in contempt of its teaching. Theirs is not a considered refusal to live up to its standards of conduct. But it is always easier to punish and cast aside than to understand. Perhaps, in the light of our limited knowledge of human behavior, the church had to deal harshly with men whose conduct seemed threatening to its security in order that it might survive. Nor is it altogether impossible, in times such as these, that there are those in the church who feel that it must tighten its belt and drive out all who fail to conform to the most rigid standards of belief and conduct. In the minds of many, that was the only way for the church to survive during the Dark Ages. There may be those who feel that this is what the church must do in the new dark night of its soul that may lie ahead. But one is entitled to question the validity of such a pessimistic view as this.

We seem to be offered a choice between a particularism in faith and morals, that limits the concern of the church to the elect, and a universalism that opens the door of Christianity, not only to those who knock, but those with courage only to stand outside, hoping to be bidden to enter. Here the church must ask itself a most penetrating question: is it sure enough of itself that it can afford to minister to those whose sexual behavior seems to threaten its security? Or, more simply put, will it continue to draw itself off from those it failed to understand, and therefore feared? Prejudice, it will be recalled, is dislike of the unlike. Homosexuals are said to be unlike other men. And of the prejudices against homosexuals, even in the church, there is no need to seek evidence.

We are able to see straws in the wind that point to the fact that the church is beginning to recognize that its dealing with all matters of sexual activity and interest is something less than adequate. Within the last couple of decades, the movement for the clinical training of the clergy has given the men undergoing it new insights into the ramifications of a problem on which the Church has been slow to move with the times. To categorize homosexuality as a nasty business and to ostracize those involved as being beyond redemption is the lazy man's way of getting something unpleasant out of sight. Such subjects are evasions of responsibility.

The Kinsey reports, the newer light thrown on sexual deviation by psychiatry, bringing the discussion of the subject to the market place, the appearance of stage plays and novels that openly talk about a phase of life hitherto tacitly ignored—all these things have brought home to the clergy the need for study that is something more than the search for authorities to bolster up age-old prejudices. In other branches of human relations, the advances of modern psychiatry have made the clergy aware of new areas for which the church must take responsibility. The sexual behavior of men and women requires study as dispassionate as that of any other type of human activity. Whether, in the nature of things, this is possible . . .

The new light that science has thrown on what is involved in our sexual concerns is commencing to dispel the gloom of the church's confusion about what is involved. Doubtless we can expect a great deal of fumbling and more than a bit of opposition from the conservatives, to whom change is unthinkable. But change is bound to come. Here is how David Roberts puts it:

"At the risk of offending some readers, I must admit that in connection with sexual matters generally, and sexual aberrations specifically, the Church has tended to be peculiarly irrelevant and floundering. There are complex reasons for this which not even a long volume on the history of theology could cover exhaustively. Suffice it to say, in a sentence, that there are ample resources in the Jewish-Christian tradition for developing a more effective understanding of the role of sexuality in human misery and beatitude, and for developing more humane, life-saving, soul-saving attitudes on a firm religious footing. In connection with their distinctive tasks, therefore, pastors and churchmen will need increasingly to learn how to cooperate effectively with psychiatrists." [4]

Save in the instances where clinically trained clergymen have cleared away these irrelevances and flounderings, those pastors who choose to speak to the condition of the homosexual will have their anxious moments. They will need to be assured that theirs are not voices crying in the wilderness. Maybe they will need occasional reassurance that they have not espoused a dubious cause, and that they speak for more than a small, and possibly suspect, group. Here, as in other realms of theology, the Church would do well to consider what is being done by the workers in the sciences. First it must decide once and for all that there is no real conflict between religion and science. The quarrel seems to be much more of words than of facts. At no time have the psychiatrists asked the church to condone sin; they do ask that it examine the human process that leads to sexual aberration before pronouncing condemnation. Perhaps a reminder is occasionally necessary that its Founder was able to find compassion for the prostitute. Understanding her sins, He forgave them. She had loved much: therefore much was to be forgiven her. Or, oversimplifying, as it may seem to some, can we not say that the new light on the sexual deviations should enable the church, as St. Augustine's adage has it, all the more to hate the sin and love the sinner?

As things stand now, a minister who undertakes to find his way out of the labyrinth of conflicting opinions about sex variance could be in a somewhat equivocal position. He has no assurance that the concern he may feel for a segment of society he is sure is in need of help may not contravene the official teaching of the institution he serves. Certainly more than a bit of tightrope walking is required if he tries to counsel those whose mode of sexual expression is against the law. This is quite vividly illustrated by Peter Wildeblood in his response to a letter he received from a Church of England clergyman who was perplexed as to how he might help a homosexual in his parish. This is what he wrote: "There are many of these cases in which the factor precipitating the tragedy has been the Law, as it now stands, or the fear of it. In my pastoral duties, I have found that one of the greatest obstacles to the guidance of homosexuals is that it is almost impossible for an adviser, whether he be a doctor, a clergyman or a teacher, to give frank advice to one of those unfortunate men without himself running into considerable danger." [5]

Mr. Wildeblood journeyed to this man's cure to discuss the problem thus raised. There he heard an obscure country vicar forthrightly put the need for the church to face facts realistically. Here is how one parish priest saw it:

"I have homosexual parishioners, and to my way of thinking, they're entitled to something from the Church in the way of help. We sit here every Sunday praying for those whose lives are made difficult through no fault of their own, and if we refuse to help such people we're plain daft. Yet nobody does anything. I don't do much myself. I can't. I'm hamstrung from the start, because quite often the best advice I can give would be contrary to the law." [6]

Here, unadorned by scientific or theological erudition, is the confession of a working pastor that he knows not where to turn. The traditional formularies of the church are meaningless to those who face a problem that cannot be overcome by admonitions to lead a better life. Even though the admonitions are reinforced with warnings of the dire fate in store, here in the form of disgrace, imprisonment and possible ruin, and hereafter in the form of hellfire and damnation, they can have little meaning for one who is caught up in forces that impel him to behave in ways the church calls sinful and the world punishes as criminal. What can a parson do for a person in that unenviable situation? And is there not some danger that the parson himself might become regarded as a member of a lunatic fringe, or, worse, that he is trying to find excuse for sin and resting on the authority of some psychiatrist rather than that of the institution that pays his salary?

One supposes, however, that those who see the need for the church to revise its views of the problem of homosexuality cannot do anything else than continue in the course they have set out for themselves. Many reforms have been kept alive, until the time came for their ultimate adoption, by the few who have been regarded as wrong-headed or even heretical. Clergymen tend to become very quiet when their ecclesiastical superiors intimate that it is best for them to cease from raising troublesome questions.

Not too long ago, no one would have thought of raising them. The laws against homosexual practices, carrying with them the most condign penalties, seemed to have the support of the whole public. There was a time, also, when that same public acquiesced in the laws that made death the punishment for innumerable offenses. But a leaven of devoted souls agitated for penal reform, despite the fact that they were regarded as bereft of their senses, or even worse. From small beginnings, much has been accomplished. The church is a cumbersome machine that takes a long time to set in motion. Perhaps it is as well, as a whole, that it does take such a long time to make up its mind; its natural conservatism saves its members from being blown about by every wind of doctrine.

Some change in the church's thought of the homosexual is long overdue. It is beginning to learn how to accept men whom hitherto it thought it could do without. And it may learn that it has a responsibility for those whose sexual behavior is such that they feel there is no place for them within its borders. After all, it has learned to seek and reach out a helping hand to those who are in other forms of trouble, sickness, want, or even crime.

Here it is not intended to predict the shape of things to come, nor to provide the church with a blueprint for the revision of its view of the homosexual. That is the task of the official formulators and teachers of its theology. We know that the church, like the world, has tried the way of judgment. They made outcasts of those who violated their laws; they shut them up in prison; they treated them cruelly; they made men's lives difficult when they returned from prison. And what has all this accomplished? It has made enemies of those who should be friends; it has made them feel their position more keenly; it has embittered them.

But a change is in sight. More and more is society looking toward the way of helpfulness as something much more realistic than the way of rejection and punishment. It is beginning to appreciate that the homosexual is just as much a casualty of the social order as any other individual it failed to understand. There is considerable likelihood that we will see some lightening of the burden when the penal laws are liberalized. That this may come about in our time seems not at all unlikely. The extent to which this will constitute an improvement is debatable; but at least it is a start.

Until the church makes a real effort to accept responsibility for the homosexual, it is remiss. Traditionally the world looks to the church for leadership and guidance with its moral problems. There is little it can do to supply that leadership until it clarifies its own position. The problem, then, can be simply stated. The church has rejected the homosexual and has cut him off from its fellowship. It has made him feel unwanted. Is this its final word? Or is there more to be said?

Thus far we have looked at the way in which the Church regards the homosexual. How do they feel about the church? Are they hostile to it? Do they feel scornful of those who sit in its high places? Do they have nostalgic feelings for it? Do they hope for a way to be found for them to return to it? Some keenly feel what they consider the unfair way the church has used them; others ignore it. Still others are sure that ultimately there will have to be a compromise. And there are a few who manage to enjoy an uneasy peace in its household through the exercise of some sort of intellectual prestidigitation. By and large, there is much less hostility to the church on the part of homosexuals than the institution has for them. Many simply stand and wait to hear its voice telling them that it is time for them to come back.

What is to be done? That something must be done is axiomatic. The trouble begins when we try to apply the axiom. How is the church to go about the business of being its homosexual brother's keeper? First, let those who lead opinion in the denominations set about reviewing the whole subject of sexual behavior. Let them inquire whether the time will have come for it to be reconsidered in the light of today's needs, and not those of a bygone generation. When Jesus told the men without sin that only they were allowed to cast a stone at the woman taken in adultery, He was, in effect, asking His hearers to inquire of themselves whether they were sure of what they were doing. They were following a custom; they were engaged in the accepted way of disposing of a woman taken in sin. This was the voice of tradition speaking. But had they ever troubled themselves to examine the soundness of the tradition. Had they asked themselves if what seemed good centuries ago might not have outlived its usefulness? How seriously, how critically, has the church examined the tradition that ostracizes the homosexual?

That is the first step—to look critically at what has too long been taken for granted. Then, if the traditional view seems to rest on an unsure foundation, the church is duty bound to reconsider it. It must seek more realistic ways to meet its responsibility for those troubled with problems of sexual deviation. Ways and means of help to do this may open themselves up if the church will avail itself of what is being done by the workers in the behavioral sciences. They will find that the opinion that the homosexual deliberately chooses a type of behavior that fails to meet social and ecclesiastical approval is an oversimplification. There is much to learn, if the church is genuinely concerned to seek and practice a more Christian acceptance of its responsibility for its homosexual brethren.

How go about meeting this challenge and this responsibility? Perhaps as good a way as any to get to the heart of the matter comes from the pen of an English writer, Caryll Houselander:

"It is time that Christians put aside the self-protective type of religion, with its interminable formalities and careful exclusions and respectable cliques, and recognize Christ and themselves in the disreputable members of the Church: the socially ostracized, the repulsive, the criminals, the insane; the drifting population of the streets and the doss-houses; the drug addicts and drunkards; the man waiting in the condemned cell to die—and the tiresome, thankless and dissolute members of a man's own household. It is time that Christians answered Cain's question, 'Am I my brother's keeper?' by more than an affirmative: 'I am more than that; I *am* my brother.' " '

CHAPTER VII

THE CHURCH AND THE HOMOSEXUAL:
PRACTICAL ASPECTS

The practical test of a religion, always and everywhere, is its success or failure in helping souls to respond to the challenges of Suffering and Sin.
— *Arnold Toynbee*[1]

When the movement for the clinical training of the clergy was in its infancy, one of its early leaders thought that the best advice to give a young homosexual living in a rural area was to tell him to move to a great city where he might become lost in the crowd. Many have acted in this wise without benefit of clergy. This has been one way of blinking a problem away that David Roberts has called the peculiar floundering and irrelevance of the churches.[2] Reluctance to come to grips with an increasingly felt human need must be seen in the light of the fact that the minister must necessarily live and work in the community. If he questions the standards of sexual morality society has long deemed inviolate, he does so at considerable risk to himself. Then, too, there is a matter that every minister must consider: possible risk to his wife and family, if he takes an unpopular stand. In this not best of all possible worlds, no clergyman can afford to ignore the consequences to himself if he should decide to go out on a limb without the support of his congregation. Furthermore, it must be taken into account that there are clergy who are helpless before a situation they fail to understand, and with which they are unable to find acceptable ways to cope.

Up to yesterday, the pastor, when confronted with the need of a homosexual, followed the example of the ostrich. The church preferred to act as though he did not exist. When a situation arose that could not be ignored, it was dealt with in the secrecy of the council chamber. The effect of this attitude on those involved needs little comment here. Scandal had to be hushed up at all costs.

Several years ago a clergyman was unfortunate enough to be arrested because of a public toilet episode. After the court finished with him, he was deposed from the ministry, given enough money to keep him for a while, and bundled off to Paris, where it was hoped he would be quickly forgotten. Another minister permitted a man to live with him whose sexual tendencies became the subject of court interest. Guilt by association operated to send the minister packing.

He was told to resign his cure and vacate his parsonage within a week. An official bulletin announced that Brother So-and-so had left the ministry to assume a position with the This-and-that Company. Within a few days a clerical conference was held, and the twittering of the brethren, as they speculated on the reasons for their former colleague's departure, was an unedifying spectacle.

It has been said that the church can somehow accommodate itself to the forger or the thief, but it is completely at a loss when it is confronted with the problem of the homosexual who has fallen upon evil days.[3] Much more is required than a few pious platitudes and the gift of a dollar or two to ease the giver's conscience. What is needed is the recognition that the church is duty bound to respond to the appeal of those in need of help. More especially must it consider its obligation to those who have some claim on it.

Here is an example of one minister's way of dealing with a situation that arose in a fair-sized town. It was a highly explosive one that could have wrecked a marriage, and perhaps a parish. Frank, a married man in his thirties, occupied a secure position. Both he and his wife came of long-established families: they had roots in the community. He owned his own home and had two cars. He was a member of the church that attracted families of wealth and social position. While he was not conspicuous for religious activity, his church attendance was more than sporadic. He had a good education.

As a matter of fact, meetings of the alumni association of his college in a distant city were the excuse he used to get away to engage in the private activities that were the occasion of his downfall.

Out of a clear sky, Frank was asked to call at the local police station. Thinking that nothing more serious was involved than a possible parking violation, he complied automatically. There he was confronted with a statement that a young male prostitute accused him of sexual intimacies. A zealous policeman, out to make a name for himself as a protector of underprivileged youth, saw a golden opportunity to bring to justice men who utilize the sexual service of boys whose affections were purchasable. He saw the chance to get his name in the headlines. Doubtless he believed that his crusade to punish men who preyed on gullible youths was a contribution to the common good. At all events, when Frank was confronted with the accusation, the Javert of vice suffered no qualms of conscience when he said that it was a minor charge, and that, if a statement were signed admitting the fact, the matter would rest there. Thinking, perhaps, that his position was impregnable, or else, hoodwinked by the policeman's easy and casual manner, Frank made no difficulties about signing a confession. Immediately he was placed under arrest. Within half an hour, he was brought before a judge and arraigned before he had a chance to consult counsel. The court imposed a fine and imposed a short jail term, which was remitted during the defendant's good behaviour.

The axe had fallen. All his family, neighbors, friends and business associates, the whole community, had been made aware of an aspect of his life he had sought for years to conceal. He was sure he faced ruin. He felt that the whole edifice of the security he had taken years to build had come toppling about his ears. So it appeared.

All sorts of pressures were put upon Frank's wife and children. They were warned that an outraged community would not permit them to stay under the same roof with one whose sexual sins had found him out. Frank thought himself helpless and friendless; he knew not where to turn. Vainly he sought for a way out. He felt trapped. His desperation reached the point where his contemplation of suicide had to be taken with a great deal of seriousness. Word of his trouble reached Frank's parish minister within a few hours after the arrest. Immediately he came forward to offer his services to salvage what he could from the wreckage. At the start, Frank's acceptance of the proffered help was half-hearted. He doubted whether the minister would be able to withstand the pressures of those ready to cast stones.

Immediate and realistic help was required. The town gossips had done their work well. Even Frank's family had seemed ready to leave him to his fate. But the minister was in the breach, fighting to reassure them of the man's essential worth. What Frank thought about himself at that time would not bear repeating. He needed to be reminded forcibly that he was worth quite a bit of trouble. Save for one aspect of his life, had he not been a good husband and father? Had he not demonstrated, time and time again, that he was in many ways a good citizen and a credit to the community? All this was forgotten by those who chose only to see a man who had committed a disgraceful offense. Once the first shock was over, the pastor was able to show the family the need for an united front against the clacking tongues of the scandalmongers.

Assured at least of the tentative support of his family and a few good friends, Frank began to take stock of his situation. What about the immediate community? What about his job? Should he pull up stakes, abandon what he had made for himself, and start anew elsewhere? As soon as word of this got about, some of the neighbors went to the family and told them that they were anxious to help in any way that they could. Several weeks elapsed, and the hostilities of the town showed signs of simmering down. The time came when what had happened could begin to be discussed with something approximating reason. Frank's employer, at the pastor's suggestion, called Frank into his office and told him that, despite what had happened, he had faith in him and in his ability to do a good job. He made it clear that the company considered it unthinkable for Frank to feel he had to leave a position he had so successfully filled. A woman in the parish called up the minister to ask what she and her husband could do to asure Frank of their friendship. She was told that it might be a better thing to make a simple gesture than a public display of confidence. A round of golf was suggested, after which Frank and his wife could be invited for luncheon.

It took a long while for the community to forget Frank's time of trouble. Another scandal arose to keep the gossips busy, and relieve the family of unwelcome attentions. The parson struck while the iron was hot. Frank was made to see the necessity for obtaining realistic help. The minister was able to spend a great deal more time, once the furor had subsided, with the family. Frank's wife and some of her relatives were a little fearful of the future. Although they could see the necessity of a united front during the worst days of the scandal, they raised many questions about the possibility of Frank returning to a course that would again cause great distress. The minister was the first to agree that safeguards had to be erected against this possibility. On the advice of his pastor, Frank arranged to see a psychiatrist. Both clergyman and doctor were able to make use of Frank's desire for conformity and status in helping him to see his need for more adult sexual behavior. Five years have passed, and Frank has felt no inclination to lapse into unorthodox ways of obtaining sexual satisfaction. Had not the church, through its ordained minister, been able to meet this overwhelming need, no one dares prophesy what might have been the outcome.

In this situation a minister rendered practical help to an individual in his time of trouble. He was quick to seize upon the most urgent need, and was fortunate enough to be able to manipulate the environment, not only of the patient, but also of his immediate family. To a lesser extent, he was able to influence part of the community. He was shrewd enough to realize that more expert help had to be called in, and he made it his business to get the patient to a good doctor. The pastor had always made himself available to those

who sought his help. In this case, he had sense enough to disregard
the convention that the minister must wait until he is called into
a situation.   Ordinarily it is in questionable taste to go charging
uninvited like a bull into a china shop. But there are times, of which
this was one, when the rule is best forgotten. Someone with common
sense had to take steps to command a situation before which everyone seemed to be helpless.

Another situation in which the minister can be of great practical
help to men in trouble is in the case of arrest for homosexual misconduct. An illustration from the files of The George W. Henry Foundation shows that it is possible for an informed clergyman to be of real
service, not only to a troubled individual, but also to the community.

Don, a poorly paid clerk, lived alone in a furnished room. He had
been arrested for indecency in a subway washroom. Don was almost
completely devoid of friends; his contact with the church was tenuous,
to put it mildly. Hic case came to notice through a kindly disposed
prison keeper calling a visiting clergyman's attention to it. This
is the story of a young man who appeared bewildered by what had
fiappened. An innocuous person, he was the son of a widowed
mother who lived in a town 500 miles away, to whom he sent a third
of his meagre salary. When the case was called, the judge asked if Don
had a lawyer. When he said that he could not afford one, the court
requested the Legal Aid Society to act for him. Apparently the
officials considered Don much too frightened to run away. He was
paroled in his own custody to await his trial

So far as the criminal offense was concerned, Don was without a leg
to stand on. There was no way to contest the charge: the boy was
guilty. A minister who was a member of the Foundation Board found
time to see Don daily until the case was scheduled to come up for
disposition. As the time for his trial drew near, Don, never too
adequate a person, became increasingly apprehensive and panic
stricken. He found it difficult to accept the assurance that there was
small chance of a New York magistrate sending an insignificant homosexual, otherwise well behaved, to prison for a first offense. It is
doubtful that he got much sleep the night before the hearing.

When the case was called, Don pleaded guilty in a scarcely audible
voice. The Legal Aid lawyer had to repeat whatever he said. The
scene in the courtroom reminded one spectator of another court in
London, where a defaulting solicitor's clerk, whose crime and punishment were so vividly portrayed in Galsworthy's *Justice,* stood to await

his sentence. Both youthful offenders were weak. True, both had committed crimes. But of evil in them . . .

The judge ordered Don to be taken away to be fingerprinted and then brought back to be sentenced. His statement that he had never been arrested before was confirmed by the records. When the time came for the judge to fix the penalty, the clergyman asked permission to address the court. He was sure the judge would want to know what he had been able to learn about Don's history, his work record, family background, and the circumstances predisposing him to the criminal act. The judge suspended sentence and told Don to keep in touch with what appeared to be a source of helpfulness.

Over three years have gone by since these events took place. Helped by the Foundation to find a more suitable job, Don decided to take a few college courses at night. As he came to accept himself and to feel that there were those whose good opinion he valued who likewise accepted him, the need for hole-and-corner sexual experiences lessened. In his case the clergyman helped to bring about a much more desirable outcome than Don could have managed for himself.

Such cases illustrate the practical aspects of the pastor's role in assisting homosexuals in their time of need. Long term aid may also be offered where this seems desirable; but it is doubtful that all are equally ready to accept this. Sometimes the clergyman must be satisfied with seeing a man through his time of crisis, even though much more needs to be done for him. There are times when a man seeks to show his gratitude by coming for counselling. Then it develops that the help that was so enthusiastically welcomed when it was the means of averting possible ruin seems less important, as the memories of one's hard times grow dim. The minister need not feel too unhappy when he sees his charge's interest slacken and attendance at the counselling sessions become irregular. Nor is there reason for surprise when his charge vanishes into outer darkness; it is perfectly natural to get as far away as possible from what reminds us of our time of trouble.

None the less, the offer of pastoral counselling should be made at all times to those who might profit from it. Counselling sometimes is the door to a fine pastoral relationship. But the counselling experiences that are voluntarily initiated seem to have a better chance of being meaningful than those that are entered into through the force of a cataclysmic situation.

In a book that does not profess to be a manual for ministers who counsel homosexuals, it is difficult to say what might be pertinent and what is gratuitous, unsought advice. What can be learned from the story of the young man who tells something of his experiences with the clergy in Chapter II of this book? It will be recalled that he feared to approach his minister, because he knew just where the minister stood in respect to sexual deviation. And the minister's position was such that it would be a desperately troubled homosexual who would approach him. Fortunately there was another pastor in the same town who took quite a different view. Unfortunately it took a prison term for the young man to find out that there were ministers and ministers. Certainly the clergy are not under obligation to advertise publicly that they are prepared to counsel homosexuals. But is not the Church as a whole under some obligation to find reasonably discreet ways of letting it be known that there is no problem of human nature and conduct beyond the willingness of some pastor to help? Certainly no institution is in a better position to say: *Nihil humanum mihi alienum;* although its ministers would be much less than human to feel that the less they had to do with some of the more unsavory aspects of human activity the better.

The long history of the church should have prepared it to understand the inevitable loneliness, bitterness and frustration of those who feel that the ministry of the church is not for them. At best viewed with contemptuous tolerance, even by many ministers, it is small wonder that there are so few well-adjusted homosexuals. To continue to acquiesce in letting well enough alone is not much more than wishful thinking that, by ignoring it, the problem of homosexuality will take care of itself. On the whole, inertia is a weak reed upon which to rely. Sooner or later, the situation gets out of hand: somebody is apt to throw a lighted match into the gun powder keg.

What is to be done? In England, pioneer work has been done by the Moral Welfare Council of the Church of England. That body had an important share in creating the demand for the appointment of the Wolfenden Committee, and it submitted several monographs that were helpful to the Departmental Committee in arriving at its conclusions. The recommendations of the Moral Welfare Council excited a great deal of interest, and they are being discussed throughout the Anglo-Saxon world. Although they deal with conditions in the United Kingdom, their applicability in this country seems obvious.

It must be made clear that the English recommendations cannot be regarded as a license to all who are so minded for wholesale indulgence in ·behavior condemned for centuries by church and state. The National Church did express its concern for people whom society had failed to understand and who were regarded as unwholesome, if not downright criminal. It pressed for study of their problem in the light of reason, rather than emotion. It was concerned for the moral welfare of a very large number of human beings who felt themselves forgotten men—men with duties to the state but with virtually no rights that anyone felt bound to respect, men who felt their position was so equivocal in the church that they preferred to get along without its ministrations. As the Church of England pressed for the understanding of the homosexual and took steps to do something about the concern it felt, so does it become increasingly evident that the American churches are beginning to feel the need to share in its concern.

The problem of homosexuality concerns many departments of learning. It involves the sciences—social, behavioral, moral. As was pointed out by Professor Karl Mannheim of the University of London, the problem is a multi-disciplinary one.' There are the contributions, among others, of psychiatry and psychology, anthropology, sociology and social work, biology and genetics, philosophy and ethics, and theology—pastoral and moral—to be considered. The Church of England chose wisely when it placed the consideration of the problem of homosexuality in the charge of its Moral Welfare Council, for the church has long been the custodian of public morals. The need for further study by all concerned, and the creation of an informed public opinion as a prerequisite to wise, sane and effective social action, is axiomatic. Is the Church ready to assume the leadership of that informed public opinion?

What can the church do? Or, better, what can it do here and now? Apart from what the church as a whole might undertake, what can the individual clergyman do when he feels the need to give concrete expression to his concern? There are two quite important areas in which the minister can be of real and lasting help. For one thing, he can hold himself available to help those homosexuals whom trouble overtakes. He can be with them when they must face a criminal charge. By going to court, helping obtain legal counsel when this seems desirable, strengthening morale, and in general seeing men through a crisis—these are real and needed services. Then, when the worst is over, he can be ready to undertake such further help as might be needed—either making himself available to those who need protracted counselling or referring them to a psychiatrist or more experienced ministerial counsellor. The well-informed minister should be able to make an educated guess when to offer his services as a guide to the perplexed; when to get them to those with greater technical skills; and when to do nothing. It is quite difficult to know how to be sure that a needy neighbor has had enough of our goodness.

Much more is required for the church to do, if it chooses to speak authoritatively to the condition of the homosexual, than helping men in trouble, important though that may be. Martin Buber does well to suggest the need for education as a beginning, if we are to understand the many and complex problems of human nature and conduct that trouble the churches. And education is required to dispel the cloud of prejudice, half-truth and downright superstition that covers men's thinking about the homosexual and his ways and works. The church may well wonder how much it may have contributed to the confusion that surrounds the problem. More than once, it has been required to cry, *"Mea culpa!"* Unless it chooses to be like the Bourbons, who never learn and never forget, the church is confronted with the need to learn and to teach.

For one thing, the church can bring the ministry of reconciliation to all who will accept it. It can make proclamation that there are within it ministers who are equipped to counsel those who choose to make use of their services. It can do much to relieve the feelings of ostracism of men and women who are persuaded that they are unwanted in the household of faith. On the Day of Atonement, the priests in the Temple at Jerusalem drove a goat out into the wilderness, laden with the sins of all Israel. The homosexual regards himself as a scapegoat who bears on his shoulders the sexual sins of the community. He needs to be reminded, in season and out of season, that there are other sins than his. Those who are troubled by what is happening in South Africa are horrified at the *apartheid* laws, that drive the natives out of the land that was once theirs into the wilderness. There seem to be some *apartheid* laws that have to do with homosexuals.

Many times in this book has reference been made to the apartness that homosexuals feel in respect to the body social, and most of the next chapter will be devoted to it. Too often the community makes them feel their lack of solidarity with it. And, as it will be shown, homosexuals respond to their feelings of ostracism by creating their own cities of refuge. Ought not those who complain about the clannishness of homosexuals wonder why they find it necessary to seek solace in this wise?

Certainly the church today offers very little. And the homosexual, if he comes to church at all, comes only to observe from afar, like the publican in the parable. When some exigent pressure drives him to approach a minister, he comes, hoping against hope, that he will find

help in his time of need. He is quite understandably doubtful if he
will be received at all. He has been so conditioned that usually he
regards himself as beyond the possibility of help from the clergy. And
this is as good a place as any to ask what the church has done and left
undone to make the homosexual feel as he does. What has the church
done to bring on its head the feeling too many homosexuals have that
it is without desire for part or lot in him?

It would appear that, just as there are homosexuals and homosexuals,
there are clergymen and clergymen. From what has been said, it
would appear that the homosexual has formed a stereotype of the
minister. Many homosexuals have been unfortunate in their choice
of ministers from whom they sought help. But there are ministers—
and their number is happily increasing—to whom men in all manner
of trouble may apply in the assurance that they will be received as
those in need of the services the church is duty bound to render.
They will get no more; but certainly no less. Yet men such as these
are in a small minority in today's church.

Fairness requires that it be stated that it would be difficult, if not
impossible, for a homosexual to find any great measure of acceptance
in the church today. It would be an unusual one in which a man
could feel at home after he had become involved in any sort of scandal,
let alone a homosexual involvement that became known. None the
less, there are clergy, even country ones in the smallest hamlets, who
are not afraid to take a homosexual in their stride and help him as they
are able.

The art of counselling those in trouble is not a new thing. It is as old
as the church. And older, too. There was a time when doctors and
priest were one and the same. Nor has the church altogether forsaken
its responsibility for the cure of souls. As a matter of fact there are
some ministers who have not quite made up their minds whether to
wear a preaching gown or a psychiatrist's white coat. We are redis-
covering the connection between body and soul. The clergy are
finding wider areas of service in which to combat the effects of illnesses
that involve problems of human behavior. They become increasingly
useful where, for one reason or another, access to a psychiatrist is
difficult or impossible. This does not mean, however, that the clinically trained man has altogether supplanted the older minister who was
able to help people out of trouble, long before it became fashionable to
tell one's troubles to the psychiatrist. Nor, by the same token, is the
psychiatrist losing his business to the pastoral counsellor. One of the
important things every minister has to learn, when he undertakes to

counsel the perplexed, is how far his training goes. He will have to learn painfully, through trial and error, when he can be useful, and when he would be better advised to have the patient put in more expert hands.

What else can the church do? Beyond the realm of pastoral care, public education and the meeting of crises in human lives, the church might help to generate a climate in which effective work can be done. The public needs to learn and the minister should teach, that the homosexual is a tragic consequence of our imperfect society. He is just as much the victim of our misapprehension as any other individual who fails to conform to the demands society makes upon its members. The difference between the homosexual and any other nonconformist is one of degree, not of kind. The church has accepted responsibility for many who are called maladjusted. The homosexual is so considered. We are not required to condone his conduct when it is offensive. We are required to make limitless efforts when he shows interest in trying, within his limitations, to live as a useful member of the body social and, hopefully, the body spiritual. All men have the right to demand that the church aid them to achieve standards of conduct that meet a greater measure of social approbation. Condemnation, threats, ostracism and imprisonment will not do this. Patience, sympathetic help and the application of the gospel of love and charity have a chance. These come within the special purview of the church. Its ministers are the duly appointed dispensers thereof.

Empirically the value of the help given by the clergy to overt homosexuals can easily be documented. When Dr. William Wolfson was working for his master's degree in psychology, he followed up the cases of one hundred men on probation for homosexual offenses.[5] These men were directed to seek aid of a psychiatrist, psychologist or minister. He also followed the histories of a like number of men who were given suspended sentences, and were not required to seek aid. Only a small number of those aided were required to return to court. Something like 20% of the unaided men came before the judges, either to answer for a new offense or for violation of the conditions of probation. The probation orders hopefully directed that those under the court's jurisdiction refrain from the behavior that got them into trouble. The Wolfson report is understandably silent as to how successful were the efforts of the men ordered to cease from following their homosexual impulses. It does state clearly and unequivocally that the men under treatment were able to control the more public manifestations of their homosexuality. They were helped to manage their lives so that it no longer seemed urgent to seek out places under police surveillance in order to find sexual companionship. That is something.

There may be those who are not satisfied with this. The perfectionists will demand to know how many men under treatment by doctors or receiving help from ministers were enabled to make such radical changes in their mode of life that they could be said to be cured. (More likely, critics of this type, when they talk about cure, mean repression.) This there was no method of discovering. We do know that the overwhelming majority of those who had the benefit of professional skills were not back in court for the same sort of offense. This is a pragmatic test: it speaks for itself.

The Wolfson report amply corroborates the strong feeling that homosexuals can make a favorable response to counselling. Unfortunately the circumstances under which the Wolfson study obtained knowledge of the cases were not the most favorable. The religious counselling or medical treatment was initiated through fear and enforced through compulsion. What would be the results of a study of a similar number of men who voluntarily sought treatment? Here one can only speculate. But the speculation must take into consideration a certain amount of wonder whether a man thinks of coming for help without some untoward circumstance spurring him.

Not every homosexual would consider applying to a minister for help. To many the church seems a persecutory force. Men such as these would do better elsewhere. Nor can every clergyman counsel homosexuals effectively. There is a popular Anglican manual for confessors that speaks quite frankly about the limits of ministerial tolerance. It advises priests to whom the topic is distasteful to direct penitents to colleagues who have become expert in this phase of the cure of souls. The reference can be made tactfully, without doing harm to the sensibilities of the individual seeking help. How many times has a physician been confronted with the same dilemma? When he feels a case is beyond his powers, he is quick to request consultation with a specialist. This is an accepted procedure among doctors, and is an everyday occurrence. Everyone is happier when the doctor recognizes his limitations. And the clergy is another type of doctor.

Nor can every minister deal with the multiplicity of problems a homosexual is apt to bring him. Some feel they do not know enough to be of genuine help. Some are too unsure of themselves to render effective aid. Some are simply too dogmatic; they only reiterate what they think it is required for them to say. The pastor who condemns and threatens is too familiar a figure to too many homosexuals. If this is the best he can do, he is well advised to avoid them like the plague. It is probably much better for a man to go without help of this sort than to have to listen to ministerial strictures about the wrath to come. There are times and places for warning. But warnings are best administered by those who can be objective about what they warn against. As Dr. Henry points out, the minister in dealing with a homosexual can be as biased, fearful and uninformed as the average layman.[6] He can confuse terms with facts. He can demand immediate repentance and reformation. All this is likely to do is to confirm the homosexual in his guilt feelings and add to his sense of ostracism.

Nowhere is it truer than in the case of the homosexual that is there such a crying need for an accepting friend. The homosexual who feels that the pastor to whom he has applied can truly accept him as a friend is well on the way to lasting help. A friend accepts his friend as he is; neither condoning what he does nor condemning him; but doing what lies within his power to help the friend to the place where his true interests are to be found.

In society's current view of the homosexual it still requires a bit of courage for a minister to counsel and help such men. He who would do this is well advised to consider the perils and dangers that may lie ahead. The married man is in a somewhat better position than his bachelor brother. The voice of Mrs. Grundy has many hearers, and there are still common scolds and gossips without number. Some may even be found in the churches, and one or two are said to wear clerical attire. The younger men who have experienced clinical training may be able to find their way somewhat more easily; because a little learning can be truly dangerous, they must listen carefully to the inner voice that warns them not to set up as clerical psychiatrists. The well-trained minister will have learned when the services of a first-aid man will suffice, and when he may safely undertake what one physician called minor psychiatry.

The older clergy and those without this specialized clinical training need not fear to serve. There is a wealth of literature at their disposal; and there are many good periodicals[7] that can be consulted, there are institutes for the clergy; and so on. There is, of course, the occasional parson who is a "natural" at helping people in trouble. Some of the older clergymen have been doing just that all of their ministerial lives. But much more is needed than good intentions to bring peace to men troubled with the sins of the flesh. And, by the terms of their commissions, ministers are charged to be ambassadors of that peace.

These are some of the ways by which the clergy are able to help men on the road to a healthy and integrated life. Today it is not too difficult for a homosexual to find those who are ready and willing to exercise the ministry of counselling and of practical help. Many more must prepare themselves to serve as guides to counsel brethren who labor under an unjust handicap that increasingly troubles men of good will.

But much more remains to be done. A start has been made. What must the church do to go further in understanding and effective action to bring about a solution of the problems of those who, "by reason of their sexual maladjustment, are in trouble with themselves, the law, or society?"[8] What is the next step? Here, again, this book does not presume to suggest a programme of action. Its function is to propose questions that seem pertinent. The answers may lie within the provenance of those who lead the Christian fellowship. To them and to all who profess and call themselves Christians the problem of homosexuality presents a challenge and a responsibility.

CHAPTER VIII

BETWEEN TWO WORLDS

For we are strangers before thee, and sojourners, as were all our fathers; our
days on earth are as a shadow, and there is none abiding.

—*Chronicles, xxix: 15*

Those who came to this country in search of an asylum in which they
might practice their religion found comfort in the society of like minded people. Newcomers from strange lands found solace among their
compatriots as together they set about the business of making places
for themselves in a land not so greatly blessed with milk and honey
as they had been led to believe. Even those who came only to
improve their fortunes found it helpful to dwell among fellow pilgrims
on the road to affluence. It is more or less axiomatic that men and
women of a common faith, of common social origins, a common
pocketbook, or even a common handicap, will tend to band together.

Caste and class, status or its lack, have a great deal to do with where
one lives. So has the color of one's skin. Even one's religious persua-
sion has a great deal to do with the place where it is possible to
find a home.

Every community has its quarters in which are housed those whose
circumstances require them to live apart from the more securely rooted
inhabitants. Usually those whom evil chance makes into second
class citizens are tucked out of the sight of the more favored members
of the community. Sometimes they are left to their own devices,
to sink or swim. Sometimes their poverty may force them unpleasantly on the notice of those who like to think of themselves as the
taxpayers. Sometimes their young get out of hand, and there are
complaints about the high cost of prisons to house juvenile offenders
from the wrong side of the tracks. And there are times when second
class citizens have their uses—as on Election Day, for example.

Once in a while a wall separates those who dwell apart from the
inhabitants of the main city. Such a wall sealed off the Warsaw
Ghetto. At other times, the wall is invisible, as is the wall that divides
Europeans and non-Europeans in Johannesburg. Not only does the
wall serve a useful purpose for its builders but it also has its uses for
those who must dwell behind it. At least it permits them
to huddle together for what solace propinquity provides. St. Paul

was very conscious of such a wall. He called it the wall of partition, the wall that separated the Church from the world.

Dwellers behind the wall of partition are regarded as strangers and sojourners, who must not be permitted to dwell too closely to the more secure elements. These justify their exclusions on the ground of possible contamination by persons whose way of life seems different. And folk who are different are always thought to be a threat to the security of those from whose ways they differ.

What sort of people are the inhabitants of a ghetto? What makes them second class citizens? Wherein are their manners and morals inferior to those who make the exclusions? One might observe superficial differences in ways of speech and ways of dress. It is possible that there are other insignificant differences. But are these necessarily signs that those who are different are evil?

Scond class citizens are obliged to pay their taxes as well as anyone else. Some complain that they get less from society for their tax money. They attend or fail to attend religious exercises; they hear good music or ragtime as their preferences dictate; and they may or may not be a little more prone to get drunk than those whose homes are on the respectable side of the wall. When evening comes, they return to their own side; then, in their private world, they may doff the masks they have worn through the day. With the next day, they resume the masks in order to emerge into the outer world for a few hours. Precisely what this shuttling between two worlds does to the commuters, one hestitates to think.

The homosexual is obliged, or perhaps he chooses, to live in a segregation of his own. In New York, for instance, several districts have found favor with those who are happier living with persons in the same boat. There are places for the poor and for the affluent, with their own conventions and their own standards of living. It is probably safe to assume that what goes on in them is kept well below the surface. Their existence is advertised chiefly by word of mouth. The knowing might be able to detect some telltale mannerisms among the residents, but it is doubtful that these would be particularly obvious to a chance observer.

The most fortunate dwellers behind the flimsy curtain are those who can make the greatest compromises with the world to which they commute. There are observers who consider that the effeminate "fairy" has somewhat the better of the bargain. He seems unconcerned with what people of other types of adjustment think about him. Certainly the more masculine appearing men, especially the married bi-sexuals, are not in too good a case, if their excursions into the *demi-monde* of their less inhibited brethren become known. It is not impossible for a sex deviate to go through life without any save the most casual commerce with the homosexual society within a society. There are men to whom the thought of anything approaching a common life, as some homosexuals lead it, is abhorrent. These are the men who under no circumstances would enter a tavern that has acquired the reputation of being a *rendezvous* of the sort known as a "gay" bar.[1] An invitation to a cocktail party would be the cause of considerable unhappiness; and the thought of being seen at a summer resort that is given over almost exclusively to the patronage of the more flamboyant element would cause any one of these circumspect souls to take to bed for a week. One young man, referring to an acquaintance who imagined himself most discreet, wondered just how much such a one really missed in his studied avoidance of those who pursued happiness a bit less inhibitedly. Perhaps the tumult and the shouting of the more ebullient spirits and their relative ease of finding congenial companionship, keep them from the necessity of seeking physical outlets in ways that invite police attention. (There is always the danger, of course, that some irate citizens will stir up the police sufficiently that they will descend in force on a place where joy becomes too unrefined.) Admittedly the price is a little high for the less robust. But consider the case of the man who professed disgust with the goings-on of the noisier *habitues* of places where suntan is acquired at small cost and who came to grief in a subway washroom.

Who of us can exist without a few minor hypocrisies? There is something to be said for the hypocrite. The word is a transliteration from the Greek noun meaning an actor. One can always hope that the actor will play his part so well that, sooner or later, actor and role become one. The business of being a homosexual necessarily makes hypocrites, (or actors, if the term hypocrite has too unpleasant a sound) of those who must wear the mask of masculinity. The most successfully adjusted homosexual is the best hypocrite, or the best actor, he can possibly be, if he is desirous of avoiding the attentions of those who look upon his sexual idiosyncrasies with jaundiced eyes. One man who made a good living on the fringes of a profession that regards a certain amount of eccentricity as an asset adopted a novel way to camouflage his libidinous needs. He dressed, spoke, and behaved so flamboyantly that he thought he was convincing everyone he was "putting on an act", albeit in rather bad taste, of overdoing the mannerisms of the most exhibitionistic of "fairies." For a time, his method of camouflage served its purpose. Ultimately its creator had to be taken to a hospital for the mentally ill. Much more can be said for the mask of masculinity assumed by those who choose to wear Grey Flannel Suits. Inconspicuous attire and the general air of men who find their way to Madison Avenue from Ivy League colleges are better passports to be carried by those who would avoid unflattering attention.

The homosexual can be likened to any member of a minority subject to the pressures exerted by those who feel the presence of an aggregation of nonconformists is undesirable. And these pressures tend to make those against whom they are directed painfully self-conscious. It would be difficult to find any number of Negroes gathered together for more than five minutes before *the* problem—in their case, the problem of color—comes up in conversation. And it is doubtful that any group of homosexuals foregathered for a social occasion in a place they consider safe could long refrain from turning the talk to the problem of homosexuality. The talk could be such as came out of the pages of a modern version of Plato's Symposium—the table talk of men whose opinions were worth hearing, as this was set down in Mr. Wildeblood's report[2] on what took place at a dinner he attended. Or it could be the frothy retailing of choice bits of scandal uttered by those who need not fear that, by taking thought, they would add a cubit to their mental stature.

The points of resemblance of the homosexual to others who belong to minorities need not be labored here. He is regarded as undesirable by those who think he needs to be "kept in his place." If he attempts to assume a somewhat larger share of life in the community, he is made to feel unwanted. In the eyes of many, he is an unassimilated member of the community. Is he unassimilable?

To the unthinking, to whom the use of stereotypes saves them the trouble of making up their minds, there is a convenient image of the homosexual available, should someone ask whether their prejudices are justified. The man who wonders if society goes too far in its condemnation of homosexuals is shown a picture of a preening, mincing, effeminate little man, whose speech, manner and appearance make him ludicrous. The inquirer is asked if he considers such an individual an ornament to any group. Who would want to associate with exhibitionists, reeking of cheap perfume, shouting feminine endearments at one another, ogling passers-by and acting as though they were caricatures of loose women? It is small wonder, then that those whose notion of the homosexual runs after this wise react to all so conditioned with feelings that are distinctly hostile. As a matter of fact no one is louder in condemnation of men such as these than the more conservative sexual nonconformists. In their thought a man like this brings disgrace on every homosexual. It is only on the surface that the exhibitionists seem to lead relatively untroubled lives. However, they seldom reach agencies that try to help those desirous of helping themselves. Since they seem able to predict the sporadic police activities against them, they are in the courts far less frequently than one might expect. They are much more nuisance than menace. Yet, by too many members of the public it is by their performances that all homosexuals are judged.

That the more conservative look askance at birds of brilliant plumage is to put it mildly. Some, with greater insight, might say: "There but for the grace of God go I". By and large, they are decidedly a minority. In a small hamlet men behaving thus would be driven out by outraged public opinion. When enough of them find their way to a great city and force themselves on general notice, they can become something of a problem. What to do about the problem is another matter.

Certainly it is easy to assume that men such as these are the only denizens of the homosexual ghetto. Once accepted, this assumption enables the lazy man to be indifferent to the fate of those who behave in outlandish fashion. But the picture bears very little resemblance to the facts. A portrait such as this bears as little resemblance to the totality of homosexuals as the picture of *Shylock* bears to the totality of Jews, or the *Emperor Jones* to all Negroes. Yet these yardsticks, emphasizing the worst characteristics, real or fancied, to be found in any minority, are used as cudgels with which to beat all members of any group singled out as candidates for the position of whipping boy. Would anyone accept Sinclair Lewis's portrait of a minister in the pages of *Elmer Gantry* as typical of all men of the cloth? Into this unedifying picture the author mixed all the worst traits he could find in all the peccant, lecherous, unlovely, clergymen he ever knew, heard of, or read about. And this he told his public—unless it was done with tongue in cheek—was what all parsons were like. There are those who for reasons they know best, choose to accept it as the verisimilitude of the clergy. Taking the worst characteristics to be found in any member of a group and holding them up as typical of all is a method of denigration that did not die with Hitler. It has still its practitioners.

Anyone who troubles himself to open a volume of history, ancient or modern, can see for himself how well this black art succeeded. Unfortunately we are not given to troubling ourselves overmuch to question what passes for the voice of authority. Hence few of us are greatly concerned about the authenticity of an official pronouncement that all conductors have big feet; something must be wrong with them. More often than not the facts turn out to be something quite different from the gospel as mediated by the denigrators of conductors.

For all that the homosexual lives behind a wall of partition that is as visible as the emperor's new clothes, he lives behind a wall just the same. And the wall serves the purpose St. Paul ascribes to it— a wall of partition. On the whole, it is easier to enter a ghetto than to leave it. It takes small effort to find one's way into the homosexual's world. Many forces conspire to keep its dwellers within its gates.

The use of the term *ghetto* can be a bit misleading. There are many ghettoes, or there are many kinds of ghetto. The inhabitants of Sugar Hill enjoy many more creature comforts than those who reside in a white slum. Yet both are ghettoes. The patrons of a fashionable mountain resort whose husbands prosper in the cloak-and-suit business may display their diamonds to one another in places that cater to what once was euphemistically called an unrestricted clientele. But human nature being what it is, the women sigh for the places where they are not allowed to play bridge. Probably they make themselves and their husbands miserable scheming how to get into places where, despite anti-discrimination laws, an Aryan certificate is a passport. Whether they will be happy when they get there is a speculation that goes beyond the competence of this book.

There are ghettoes for the rich as for the poor. Their inhabitants are collected by force. The force need not be the exercise of naked power. Many motives can impel men and women to take their places among their suffering brethren. When Henri Bergson chose to stand in line with the Parisian Jews and receive the armband that Hitler hoped to make a badge of infamy, he was not driven into a place on the line. For years he had lived in Paris without giving much thought to the outward religious observances of orthodox Judaism, from which he had long parted company. It was very doubtful that the Germans would have taken very many steps to have him enrolled forcibly—or otherwise. Yet Bergson felt it necessary to "stand up and be counted:" he could not do otherwise. Likewise, under conditions of stress, a very light colored Negro might feel that he must make proclamation of his kinship with his brethren of darker complexion. It is not easy to

enumerate the reasons that impel one to take his place with those who
seem despitefully used. Was it not said that the blood of the martyrs
is the seed of the Church? A persecution of homosexuals would probably show some very interesting aspects of human character. Perhaps
it would bring out a great man's weakness; perhaps it might bring out
the greatness in the obscure; and it would almost certainly provide the
spectacle of men running for cover.

Can one belong to two kinds of rejected minorities at the same time?
There are, for instance, Jewish homosexuals and Negro homosexuals.
The wall that separates the homosexual from those whose adjustment is different can be raised just as high in a Jewish quarter or a
Negro quarter as it can in a white middle-class community. It is
not at all difficult to put up a wall within a wall. Is the lot of homosexuals any happier among Jews and Negroes (let us ask) than among
the dominant groups? At first glance, it might appear that, realizing
the struggles of those who must contend with the handicap of identification with such a group, there might be greater understanding of the
homosexual's plight. But this is not necessarily so. The pressures
that impel members of minorities to struggle for acceptance could well
cause them to be less tolerant of their members whose conduct might
jeopardize them in their striving for the approval of the majority.
They fear anything that would seem to increase their undesirability
in the eyes of the makers of opinion. Hence there are Jews and
Negroes to whose security the presence of a homosexual in their midst
is a very real and present danger. There are, of course, Jews and
Negroes who feel no need to bask in the light of general approval,
and who are keen to recognize the homosexual's plight and help as
they can. But, by the same taken, there are some homosexuals who
share the prejudices of those who set the standards to such an extent
that they would be mortified to feel that a Jew or a Negro was able to
have compassion on them.

One wonders what useful purpose is served by exposing the private
lives of one's neighbors to the public gaze. Apparently the price
one pays for being poor, or sick, or in trouble, is the attention of the
curious. Sometimes those who bestow their unwanted attentions force
them on their objects in the name of doing good. Practically nothing
is done to protect the unfortunates whom evil chance places at the
mercy of the official or semi-official inquisitors, or, for that matter, from
the ordinary run of busybodies. The convicted criminal may be told
that the investigations of his private life by the probation officer will
enable the judge to come to a more just decision when he sits to fix

punishment. With all the facts of the man's life before him, it is said, the judge can have a better understanding of the case. Of course nothing is said about what will happen if the prisoner tells the officer that it matters not a tinker's dam to him whether the judge understands or fails to understand the case. The seeker of home relief has a very lively notion of what will happen unless he tells the investigator all that is required about himself, his ancestors and his descendants—not to mention highly circumstantial evidence of the financial resources of his fourth cousin in Kokomo, Indiana. The complicated life of the twentieth century citizen is lived in a goldfish bowl. Once he invites the attention of officialdom to himself his right to privacy has gone the way of all flesh.[3]

Prejudice against the homosexual being what it is, he can expect very little protection from the importunities of all sorts of investigators. He can be sure, however, that the details of the mechanics of his sexual performance will not appear in the public press. And that is about the limit of any right of privacy he may think he has. The novels that purport to tell of what takes place in the "gay" world are obliged to draw a curtain before the bedchamber. It is just as well that there are a few limitations imposed on what goes on in the name of literary art. Here, again, one can see many objections to censorship; but it is a little difficult to improve the taste of those who would publish what many find objectionable in order to line their pockets. On the other hand, no one compels his neighbor to read what he finds disagreeable.

There is a world into which homosexuals retreat. In it they are just as much entitled to privacy as the dwellers of Harlem or the East Side of New York City, or, for that matter, a fashionable suburb. Once more the matter of taste comes up. It is highly questionable what good is accomplished by the conductors of sightseeing expeditions, even though they are called good-will tours, when they lead the curious to see human misery in slums. The preface to an English book, professedly written by a homosexual, tells how sightseers were taken to a tavern to see the "gay boys" cavorting. Profit seekers found it possible to cash in on the desire of the vulgar to view the antics of freaks. Within a few years, a book, allegedly written by a clergyman, told how he accomplished the cure of a homosexual. In the course of treatment, he took the reader on a slumming expedition into what passes for life in the more lurid parts of homosexual society. This he may have done in order to let the readers see from what depths of depravity he was able to rescue his patient. Or else he

thought it necessary to show how hard he worked, and what frightful
orgies he was obliged to witness at second hand in order to accomplish
his purpose. Supposedly the book represented a contribution to
science. Its style was different from what usually appears in print
as an example of scientific method.

History has a way of repeating itself. The writer of the Epistle
to the Hebrews, nineteen hundred years ago, had occasion to address
a letter to some strangers and sojourners in Rome who were in the
process of becoming a Christian Church. This is how he spoke to
their condition: "But recall the former days, when, after you were
enlightened, you endured a hard struggle with sufferings, sometimes
being publicly exposed to abuse and affliction, and sometimes being
partners with those so treated."[4] Whoever wrote that could have been
thinking of any minority group trying to find a foothold for itself.
Its members had to learn, chiefly by trial and error, their place in the
scheme of things.

Sometimes enlightenment can be a very painful thing. What
happens when a Jewish child or a Negro child, first learns that his
different religion or his different race marks him off from his play-
mates? What can his mother tell him—when he comes home in tears,
to be comforted? How does it affect one to go through life knowing
that those who are somewhat different look down upon him? Is this
something that has to be accepted? How does he keep from being
embittered? What is there to say to modern strangers and sojourners
who must dwell apart? Some have the rare good luck to remain
ignorant of their differences from other men until they are well into
adolescence, or even manhood. At least they were spared a painful
childhood.

There are those who profess to go through life impervious to that
which marks them off from the common life. They claim that their
sexual differences from the rest give them no trouble. Certainly they
must be aware of what happens to those less fortunate, although they
seem able to close their eyes to the possibility of arrest or blackmail.
There were German Jews who were able to persuade themselves
that Hitler's atrocities were meant only for less desirable East Euro-
pean Jews. After all, Russian and Polish Jews were more than a bit
undesirable; some were downright uncouth. How strangely familar
that sounds! Other minorities have sought to assimilate themselves.
Sometimes their attempts to pass unnoticed were successful; just as
often they brought grief to those for whom life was a nightmare of

concealment. They sound like the man who, being dragged off to the station house, keeps shouting, "You can't do this to me!"

The writer of the Epistle must have had in mind what is nowadays called guilt by association. Even those who engage in helpfulness must reckon with it. The unmarried psychiatrist or psychologist with too many homosexual patients in the view of some scandal monger can be a sitting duck. And there are homosexuals who are not above a juicy morsel who can ruin a reputation by suggesting that a doctor who goes out of his way to be helpful might have some very personal reasons for doing more than what the strict requirements of duty warrant. Certainly the unmarried clergyman who tries to help homosexuals is well advised to be like Caesar's wife. Kindness can always be misinterpreted, and the tongues of gossips can cause untold misery.

It is not at all difficult to understand how a homosexual consults his fears when a friend falls on evil days. Is not the society that lumps all homosexuals and those who know them as partners somewhat to blame when a man takes to calculating the risk when he is called upon to stand by a friend in trouble? The notion of guilt by association can just as easily make one man a homosexual because he has homosexual friends as it may make another a communist because he might be seen hobnobbing with those whose political views are suspect. None the less, the homosexual who cannot afford to have attention directed to him is well advised to be the soul of circumspection. The writer of the Letter to the Hebrews had this in mind when he spoke of the vulnerability to attack of the little group that was in process of becoming a church. Let them conduct themselves as Christians, and their behavior would be viewed with suspicion by the more dissolute Romans. All a demagogue needs to inflame a mob, as has been suggested so many times, is to call attention to a few such differences. The appeal to prejudice is timeless.

Because many sections of the community regard the homosexual as one who leads a precarious, semi-criminal existence, he is regarded as fair game by anyone in search of a scapegoat. It is more than twenty years since we observed that the homosexual lived under what we called an unholy trinity of fears—of the police, of exposure, and of the blackmailer. And we wondered then, as we still wonder, which is the worst of the three. Perhaps it is meaningless to speculate about the matter. The fear of exposure is bad enough; but everyone has a skeleton or two tucked away in a closet. The fear of the police is, of course, disquieting, yet after one is arrested one can at least come to terms with the consequences one has to meet. But the blackmailer is insatiable. His threats and menaces end only when his victim is bled white or kills himself. He seems far and away the greatest of the fears with which every homosexual must live; even though there are some who seem to be able to ignore his existence. Even though fear of exposure and arrest are frightening, their effect seems less devasting than the never-ending fear of when the blackmailer, like the horse leech's daughters, will cry: "More, more!" These are the keys to the kingdom of the homosexual.

It is a strange world—the homesexual's Island Within.⁵ At its portals sit the three weird sisters, brewing their devilish draught of fears. Those who enter must quaff a cup of the witches' potion. And it is a strong brew indeed. Some say it tastes like nectar; others call it strong poison. Nor can any one tell when it will take effect. Some may go through life without ever having to pay for their drink; others may suffer a tragic experience within minutes after passing through the doors.

There is no easy way to describe a land about which travellers bring back different and contradictory tales. Some call the homosexual's world a paradise of pleasure; others would inscribe over its gates the words: "All hope abandon, ye who enter here!" It is a world that beggars description. We are given some clues to its nature by a man who paid the toll the guardians of the gates demand of those entering it. Peter Wildeblood had to serve a term in a British prison in order to know what there was to that universe he calls an underworld. He says that he who would explore it "is handicapped by the fact that no maps to it exist".

"It would take more experienced talent than mine to do justice to this theme. As a result, however, of my prosecution and imprisonment, I have one small qualification to put forward; I have been on both sides of the fence which separates Society from its misfits, the world from the underworld, and the no-man's-land which surrounds it is a territory which I have crossed and re-crossed many times.

"It is a bare and comfortless place, in which the only subjects of interest are human beings. In this it resembles the exercise-yard of a prison, where there is nothing to look at except the faces of other prisoners and nothing to hear except the shuffle of their feet on the concrete and the sound of their voices, eternally complaining of the world's injustice, eternally spinning webs of words in which, from time to time, one may discern a shining drop of sudden truth. The population is not a constant one; new prisoners arrive every day, and others, perhaps only temporarily, are released, and sometimes the yard is deserted except for the stray cats and the pigeons that scavenge along the window-sills.

"A prison block, like any other social organism, has its different levels. Each man lives in a private cell, a small world of his own from which he cannot escape, except to join the others in the yard. If you stand outside a prison, you will hear the prisoners shouting to each other through the windows, but the windows are small and the walls are thick, and it is almost impossible for a man to hear his neighbour's voice.

"This book is not about prison, but most of the men and women in it are prisoners. They are not enclosed by bricks and mortar but by their circumstances and their desires; some are the prisoners of their upbringing, some of their poverty, others of their wealth; there are the prisoners of the flesh and of the spirit; some who, through greed or malice, have imprisoned themselves hold the key that would liberate them from their cells. I walk with them in the exercise yard, and at night I listen to their voices calling from the windows, desperate but unheard.

"The prison is not always a gloomy place. There are times when it is full of laughter, and one forgets the surrounding walls. Nor are the people in it entirely bad; no-one in the world is entirely good or bad. The prison visitor may have his vices, and the man in his cell has his virtues. It is the duty of the chronicler who stands in the yard to portray these men and women as they are, ignoring the descriptions which the warders have pinned upon their doors."[6]

From many sides there will come criticism that quoting, with seeming approval, Mr. Wildeblood's parable of the homosexual world as a prison is adopting too gloomy a view. The objectors are in somewhat the same position as the psychiatrist in a midwestern prison who wrote to complain that the analogy between homosexuals and members of misunderstood and ill-treated minorities, such as Jews, was ill-chosen, to say the least. Jews, he insisted, were law-abiding citizens and the homosexuals were criminals. It all depends upon who sees a process that is capable of description up to a point, but not of definition.

Regardless of how one may view it, there is a world to which every homosexual attaches himself. It is neither paradise nor prison; but there are probably times in the lives of its citizens when it partakes of the aspects of both. To review the incidents of life in that world is doing a disservice to the overwhelming majority of those who have had to come to terms with it—and that through no deliberate act or choice of their own. Nowadays it seems fashionable to regale the readers of all sorts of publications with descriptions of the heights of human beatitude and the depths of human depravity. Those to whom that sort of literary fodder is acceptable are not unlike the Russian *grande dame* of Czarist days who wept at the misfortunes of the heroine in a comfortable theatre box, while her coachman shivered outside in the cold, waiting on the open seat of her sleigh, until the actress dramatically expired or started on the way to living happily ever after. Human misery is not made one bit less miserable by the tears of the sentimentalists, the stares of the curious, or the snickers of the prurient.

How can we get to the heart of the matter? Trying to assign blame for a situation that needs only to be stated to make its need for correction patent is probably of much interest to those who see only black and white. But certain facts are ineluctable. Men are lumped together in the popular mind as fit only for consignment to an underworld, as Mr. Wildeblood calls it, where their presence will give a minimum of offense. No one troubles himself overmuch to question the justice of the arrangement. This is the way it has always been. Why not let well enough alone? Why should society trouble itself about what happens to those individuals who may be somewhat unfortunate, but who, in any case, by their conduct, have put themselves beyond the pale?

These are questions that can be raised in respect to any minority group against whom society has erected its wall of partition. Those who would build higher walls must bear in mind that the wall affects not only those it shuts out but those who live on what they consider the pleasanter side. No doubt the wall serves its purpose for a time. The Chinese Wall kept the barbarians on their own side for a long while. But no wall lasts forever. Short of killing them off, there is very little that can be done to effectuate a permanent solution of the problem of how to exclude any set of undesirables, or those considered undesirable. Sooner of later, the wall is bound to come tumbling down. And then what?

All over the world, men are in rebellion against the discriminations practiced by conquerors who have made the inhabitants of distant possessions into second class citizens. One set of imperialist governments cut its losses by facing the inevitable, through granting independence to subject peoples. What is going to happen with respect to the new tide of imperialism that offers a sugar-coated pill to disguise a new variety of slavery is something we may see in our time.

Ordinarily the Roman Empire is not considered a model of good government. In one place it did show remarkable wisdom. When it became increasingly evident that a little group of men from a small corner of the Italian peninsula were not numerous enough to rule the world, Rome extended the rights of citizenship—first to all Italians, and then quite gradually to all within the conquered lands who made themselves useful or who had the price to purchase the right to become Roman freemen. It is far easier to govern a society without second-class citizens than to rule over helots cowed into submission. Making it possible for all within its borders to be free members of a free commonwealth is the only practical way of putting an end to the troubles of any society that considers some of its members inferior beings.

We are told in the Scriptures that "The same stone which the builders refused, is become the head-stone in the corner." [7]

Who can tell what contributions to the common life might be made by those who are denied the opportunity to make them because they dwell apart as strangers and sojourners?

Unlike the comfortable Victorian England of Gilbert and Sullivan, the land wherein they sojourn as strangers is not peopled by grown-ups who once were "every little boy or girl born into this world alive." They found their way deviously into the kingdom of the homosexual; they drifted into it imperceptibly; or they were thrust in. And once in, they have very little choice about what they do there. Within limits, they may be "a little liberal, or else a little conservative." But force of circumstances seems to govern even this. Of such is the homosexual's Island Within.

CHAPTER IX

THE HOMOSEXUAL AGAINST HIMSELF

The fundamental difference . . . lies ultimately in the old conflict between liberty and discipline, or rather in the degree to which each is valued. The most ardent lover of liberty has to admit that his own personal inclinations cannot form a satisfactory standard of conduct. He must in certain matters subjugate his will and his inclination to the prevailing laws and principles and beliefs, and he must sacrifice his private aims and desires to the common interest even when his reason and will may not be convinced. That is a simple matter of compromise.

—*A. C. Benson[1]*

When the *Mayflower* dropped anchor off Plymouth Rock, the Pilgrim Fathers drew up a code to guide them as they established a new commonwealth. In the Mayflower Compact, they hoped to set forth the rules that would enable them to live the good life. It expressed their highest ideals for the government of men who would live together in a theocracy—to them the perfect state.

Man seems always to need authoritative statements to tell him what he must do. When the law is laid down for our guidance we are dissatisfied. We become unhappy because the rules demand more than we are able to give. Between our ideals and their attainment there is a great gulf fixed. This is a perfectly natural state of affairs. In the moral realm, the difficulties grow out of hitching our wagon to a star. We need the book of rules; yet we rebel when we must come to terms with it; we denounce it as unworkable. But where there is no vision the people perish. Our struggle with the rules sets up all sorts of difficulties within ourselves. Perhaps there is enough of this sort of trouble evident for W. H. Auden to call ours the Age of Anxiety.

Scholars who like the cyclical theory of history might try to show that we are living in a time like that foreshadowing the Fall of Rome. They can point to what seems to be the decline of manners and morals, the breakdown in religion, the undue emphasis placed upon wealth and material things, the disrepute into which authority has fallen, and the loss of respect for traditional ways of doing things. Can ours be the age of Nero *redivivus?* A hasty glance about us would show many points of resemblance between life in Rome in the year A. D. 62 and what goes on in New York in 1962. It takes considerable courage to set up in opposition to Mr. Auden; but, as one views the spectacle, perhaps a better name would be the *Age of Expectancy*. Everyone is vaguely, or quite clearly, unhappy with things as they are; and all of us seem to be looking for a vóice to speak to our condition with genuine authority. Enough voices compete for a hearing. Some are harsh and strident; others are gentle and persuasive. What assurance have we that the brazen voice is not that of a monster, or the gentle one a siren song?

Meantime men muddle along as best they can. It is the rare individual who goes through life without regrets. What of the opportunities we have missed? Despite the knowledge that it is futile to cry over spilt milk, who of us is without sins, negligences and ignorance to bemoan? Here there is a very real danger of overdoing, and we can get into all kinds of trouble. Catholic theologians have a name for this: they call the preoccupation with vain regret for petty offenses scrupulosity. A good example of this comes from the story of the Pear Tree in St. Augustine's *Confessions*. We are told how, when he was a younster in his native town in North Africa, Augustine and a few choice spirits whom, in middle life, he called "lewd companions", went out in search of adventure. The boys saw a pear tree that struck their fancy. They stripped it bare; and, after eating their fill, they threw the fruit they dared not eat, lest they become sick, to the hogs. Of course it was an act of vandalism—of the sort that those with commerce with 'teenagers' today have considerable knowledge. But was Augustine right in bewailing his conduct a quarter of a century after the event, when he dolefully cried, "O Lord, my God, I inquire what in that theft delighted me?"

St. Augustine's guilt feelings over what was obviously a boyish prank strike a responsive cord in many homosexuals. Society, through its lawmakers, be they civil or ecclesiastical, prescribes rules of conduct making ways of expressing the sexual impulse not in accordance with the orthodox manner illegal and immoral. Those who offend against the moral codes often get into worse trouble with themselves than they do with the authorities. Still worse is the fate of those who, like Augustine, endlessly persist in lamenting their course. On the one hand, they must deal with the compulsion to act in accordance with what they feel to be their natures. On the other, they realize that what they do is offensive to many of their fellow men. The law makes what they do criminal, and the religiously inclined among them are convinced that theirs are lives lived in sin. The sort of conflict this sets up within oneself requires little amplification. It needs only to be suggested to realize how it can affect the personalities of those involved.

On the lowest terms, guilt feelings operate as a bar to the good adjustment of the individual to society. Some men deal with them by professing to deny their existence. It is quite possible that some can do a fairly good job of shutting them in a dark closet. That does not obviate the fact that society shuns the sexual nonconformist; and that is a fact which, with all the will in the world, cannot be wished away. It requires a very special kind of fortitude—some might call it foolhardiness—to go through life sublimely indifferent to what the world thinks.

It is difficult to see how a man whose conduct flies in the face of opinion for which, at one time or another, he had some respect, can be said to be at peace with himself. Worldly success might bring him a certain amount of immunity. The more he is able to accomplish in the way of achieving success, the more vulnerable he becomes. The greater his position, the more he feels called upon to defend it. If, in the process, his fears lead him to develop some undesirable traits, what happens is at least understandable.

The homosexual did not reach his unenviable position through his own unaided efforts. It is quite easy for the scoffers and scorners to engage in his denigration. But let them remember that they and their ancestors must bear more than a little responsibility for what has happened to him. The view in which the homosexual is held by the unthinking did not emerge, suddenly and full-blown, like Pallas Athena, from the head of Zeus. It took a long time for it to be planted, tended and watered. Well nurtured as it is today, this social disesteem of the homosexual must be considered as much as what he has done that is culpable, when we seek to understand the conflict within himself and with the community. Many psychiatrists believe that not a few of the homosexual's guilt feelings are due to forces beyond his control.

If he will reflect for a moment, a man can put himself in a somewhat more comfortable position in respect to the guilts that arise out of his sexual deviation. As Sherwin Bailey points out, homosexuality in itself is a state: it is morally neutral. The minute the state is translated into act, the act becomes sinful in the eyes of the church, and criminal before the law. As Dr. Henry sees it, desire is universal.[2] What one does about it is another matter. When, at ninety, Mr. Justice Holmes saw a bevy of pretty girls coming down a Washington street, he sighed for the time when he was seventy.

In our attempt to ascertain what is involved in the homosexual's war against himself, it must be recalled that only the strictest sort of moral rigorist would consider his situation as one altogether of his own making. But even the most liberal moralist cannot give a blank check to men who are willing to use it as justification for the evasion of any sort of responsibility for the use or misuse of their sexual capacities. There are those who are quite ready to believe that whatever they do will be condemned: everything they do is wrong, and they think and act as though theirs is a hopeless situation.

If it is considered that some attention should be paid here to the ethics of sexual acts, our starting point must be that all human beings are ends in themselves. They are not to be used as means. Father James O. S. Huntington, whom many regard as a great Anglican saint, once said that the sex act was especially grievous when it degraded oneself or another. The sin consisted in using one's neighbor as an instrument to provide a moment's fleeting pleasure. Here, then is the ethical imperative. Every human being is an end in himself; to use him otherwise is to deprive him of the dignity that is rightfully his. By the same token, no one must permit himself to be used as a means to gratify another's search for pleasure. He must answer for what loss of his own dignity such an act entails. Not to have a decent respect for one's dignity carries with it tragic consequences.

All this is well put by Dr. George W. Corner, of the Rockefeller Institute, when he says: "To involve another human being in the powerful emotional tensions of sex without regard to the other's welfare and lasting happiness is indeed immoral. The real sin is to indulge transient desires without concern for order, beauty and honor."[3]

We can see the effect of indulgence without thought of consequence in the pathetic individual called the "fairy." Here is one who seems to lack any vestige of dignity. Very early in life, he became so aware of rejection that he threw up the sponge. To him nothing seems to matter. He regards himself as a scapegoat; and, by his conduct, he invites whatever is meted out to him in the way of scorn and abuse. Within him dwell at one and the same time acceptance and defiance of the world's opinion of his ways and works. He has become a symbol of defeat.[4]

With the possible exception of the "fairy," the homosexual as was pointed out, is obliged to live two, or even more lives.[5] First there is his public life—at work or as he goes about the occasions of an ordinary citizen. When he ventures forth in the morning, as was suggested in the last chapter, he carefully dons the mask of conformity.

This he retains until the time comes when he can "be himself" and take his ease among those among whom he feels no need for disguise. Perhaps this is one of the reasons why the homosexual tavern, the "gay bar", enjoys such popularity. In places such as these (and here one thinks of a beach that has acquired international notoriety as a homosexual *omnium gatherum*), he can act in uninhibited fashion with scant fear of consequences. In the company of the sympathetic, he can put aside for a while the restrictions that convention places upon what he considers his freedom of expression.

It is a moot question whether such an escape hatch serves a useful purpose. On the one hand, it can rescue some from a humdrum existence among the more conventionally disposed. But the bell tolls at midnight and the homosexual Cinderella must leave the ballroom for an humble cottage. What happens to the personalities of those who ride that sort of merry-go-round? There are men who eschew the perfervid, artificial society of the homosexual's Never-never land and are able to live without this crutch. For some escape may be a necessity; for others it is a dangerous drug. None the less, it is questionable whether the business of managing to be a citizen of two worlds simultaneously is productive of good mental health. One wonders which aspect of such a personality is Dr. Jekyll and which is Mr. Hyde.

Again and again, one hears of homosexuals referring to their universe as the "gay" world. One wonders about the authenticity of the gaiety. Some homosexuals regard themselves as carefree souls. Many men, and especially those who regard themselves as superior citizens of a Mad Hatter's universe, find it necessary to wear a mask of hardness, brittleness, aplomb, indifference. Whether, as one suspects, the mask covers a multitude of fears on the part of the wearers to come to term with themselves, it is hard to say. Perhaps they have worn it so long that it has become part of them. Such men as these find their places in the sun as arbiters of fashion and taste. They seem to act like aristocrats of the court of Louis XVI waiting for the tumbril to take them to the guillotine. It is highly questionable that they are on as good terms with themselves as they would like to have it appear.

Many have undertaken to describe what goes on in the homosexual Vanity Fair. From reading the accounts or listening to the talk of some modern Petronius, it would be easy to imagine oneself in a strange new world. But there are other universes just as strange. Consider the young who speak the almost unintelligible language

known as "jive" or "be-bop." Or consider the thoughts, the manners
and the morals of those who call themselves the "beat" generation, although these seem ready to be stored away in the museum of forgotten
fads. Their speech requires an interpreter. And one supposes that the
"beatniks," in their brief day, were at a bit of a loss to apprehend, much
less comprehend, the "squares" who professed to speak the Queen's
English and refused to throw the amenities of life overboard. Com-
munication between the two worlds was a trifle difficult, to say the
least.

The business of tightrope walking must necessarily affect the personalities of those who do the balancing act. The performer could
better himself immeasurably if he were to take a somewhat more
optimistic view of his situation. He is not quite the lost soul he
sometimes thinks he is. Too many homosexuals are persuaded that
there is no room for them in the ordinary world. Hence they retreat into private worlds, from which they emerge as little as possible.

This sort of dual citizenship presents many hazards, especially when
it is necssary to keep one's friends in both worlds a healthy distance
apart. Some homosexuals are lucky enough to find jobs where a few
eccentricities can be shrugged off as manifestations of artistic tem-
perament. Most men are not so fortunate; they lack an ivory tower in
which they can thumb their noses at the world with impunity.

The fact remains that the people called normal make the rules.
He who is able to make the greatest compromises is least likely to get
into trouble with himself or those who disapprove departures from
the accepted ways of doing things. The applicability of this home
truth goes beyond sexual nonconformists. All of us live in some sort
of society; and few societies are willing to let their members do
whatever pleases them. The wisdom of a certain amount of surface
conformity must commend itself to any who think it important to live
with one's neighbors with a minimum of friction. Unless one is making
a special effort to court martyrdom, it should be possible for the
homosexual to make some compromises with the world. So long as he
manages to avoid calling attention to himself, he is not apt to be
bothered overmuch. Admittedly advice of this sort is not soothing
syrup for exhibitionists.

Sooner or later, most of us come to realize the folly of beating our
heads against stone walls. This is a fact that no one who thinks
conformity unimportant likes to hear. It is obvious that those who are
not able to say very much about what the majority put in the book of
rules have to play the game as the book spells them out. The more

nearly the game is played in accordance with the book, the more comfortable will the players be. This may seem cynical, but it has more than a little common sense to commend it. There is an old, old story about someone who came to Thomas Carlyle and told him that Margaret Fuller had accepted the universe. The sage of Chelsea pondered this for a while and asked, "What the devil else could she do?" In order to come to some sort of terms with himself, the homosexual has got to take the fact of the universe and its opinions into account. So long as he chooses to live in a private cloudcuckooland, he must remember that his is a glass house at which small boys and their unkind elders can be expected to throw stones. If he would come to some sort of terms with himself, he must be willing to make the effort to see himself as others see him.

And few others see the homosexual as helpless as he sometimes sees himself. Because the world may have buffeted him about, he is apt to do very little about improving his condition. He feels the cards to be stacked against him. Should one believe that?

A blind youth knocked at Dean Hawkes' door, seeking to be admitted to Columbia College. He told the Dean about his ambitions, about his good scholastic record at a school for the blind, and about his hope to be permitted to try his luck along with the sighted students. The Dean gave him some practical advice: "You are a handicapped boy. It is not enough for you to be good; you must be better than good." This seems a hard saying, and many homosexuals refuse to admit that they are handicapped. Dr. Bailey suggests that many resent the fact that they are regarded as unfortunate. The fact remains that the homosexual labors under some rather severe handicaps. What is called discrimination is practiced just as much against him as against Jews and Negroes. There is no use blinking that. To say otherwise is to deny the obvious. It would, of course, be very pleasant if there were no problems of adjustment to be faced by any of us in the quest for our places in the social order. The facts fail to bear out such a notion. If he is at all realistic, the homosexual must accept the universe that is full of obstacles to be overcome. This seems self-evident.

Facing facts can be an unsettling business; but we cannot wish the unpleasant ones away. Daydreams may help, but woe betide the man who persuades himself that they will come true. Sooner or later comes the awakening. This is how Dr. Hamilton Wright Mabie pictured it at the turn of the century:

"One may dream as he pleases, for dreams lie outside the sphere not only of the actual but of the possible. A man ought to hope however, for those things only that lie within his reach. That reach may be immensely extended and hope involves this enlargement of reach rather than those magic happenings which bring fortune, fame, and influence to our doors. A rational hope ought to rest in the expectation that one may have the strength to pursue and overtake these difficult and elusive rewards, rather than in the expectation that they will seek him out. For hope involves the possibility of realization, and must be shaped, therefore by the molding touch of an intelligent purpose.

"Men are prone to disregard this law and so transform their dreams into hopes; and when those dreams are shattered by a rude awakening, they inveigh against the order of life and permit themselves to sink into the slough of depression. As a matter of fact, they have not suffered any real disappointment; what has happened has not been a denial of their desires, but the disclosure of the unreality of those desires. No man has a right to hope for things which he does not earn, and no wise man strives to earn things which are clearly out of his reach; the blind man cannot hope to paint pictures, the dumb man to sing, or the lame man to run; and no man has ground for disappointment if things which he has not earned, or cannot earn, do not come to him.'"

Escape into fantasy can be used by a homosexual who would postpone coming to terms with an inexorable world. Yet sooner or later the bill is presented for payment. Worse than that, living in a realm of fantasy helps him lose sight of a sense of responsibility. Of course it is understandable how those who think the world too much for them seek to escape from it and from the responsibilities one must assume when he is born into it. He will find it easy to convince himself that whatever he does is wrong, and will be held against him. Why should he trouble himself with any feelings of responsibility?

The lack of a sense of responsibility is not confined to homosexuals. It is part of the indictment by the elders of the younger generation. It furnishes topics for the preachers, grist for the mills of commencement orators and ammunition for the croaking Cassandras who are convinced, and seek to persuade the rest of us, that the world is headed for destruction. Perhaps what seems to be irresponsibility on the part of homosexuals is but a reflection of the *Zeitgeist*. None the less the appearance of irresponsibility on the part of homosexuals helps their critics to indict them as primarily devoted to the pursuit of pleasure. They do not find it hard to demonstrate, at least to their own satisfaction, that all who follow after unconventional sexual patterns are hedonists. For that reason homosexuals and many others would do well to pay some attention to what Dr. Nelson Glueck has to say about our responsibilities in the world:

"I have learned that trying to find a carefree world involved me in an endless chase in the course of which the opportunity for happiness and the happiness of attainment are all too often lost in the chase itself. It has become apparent to me that I cannot wipe out the pains of existence by denying them, blaming them largely or completely on others, or running away from them.

"The elements of weakness which mark every person cannot absolve me from the burdens and blessings of responsibility for myself and others. I can magnify but never lessen my problems by ignoring, evading or exorcising them. I believe that my perplexities and difficulties can be considerably resolved, if not completely overcome, by my own attitudes and actions. I am convinced that there can be no guarantee of my happiness except that I help evoke and enhance it by the work of my hands and the dictates of my heart and the direction of my striving.'"

In addition to the need for a sense of purpose and a deepened sense of responsibility, the homosexual, like every other human being, must somehow be helped to a sense of security. Somehow, also, he must find his fair share of affection. These needs—for security and affection —are considered to be among the greatest of human needs. Living as he must, with so many things to threaten his security, it is small wonder that immediate gratifications may seem a moment's substitute.

Unless he can commence to discriminate between what really is security and what is a spurious substitute, there is little chance of attaining it. Make no mistake about the matter. There is no royal road to learning how to make this discrimination. Nor can it be done by everyone in the same way: no two human beings are alike.

And the homosexual must learn, somehow or somewhere, that the pursuit of sex for its own sake has very little to do with satisfying his need for affection. Everybody needs affection—great quantities of it. None of us are above needing to be wanted and loved. All of us need to feel that we are important to other souls. We flourish best when we realize that there are others to whom we matter. It is the rare man or woman who can sing with the Miller on the Dee: "I care for nobody, no, not I; And nobody cares for me."

Self-sufficiency is an excellent thing, and the psychiatric textbooks contain many warnings of the evils of over-dependence. Somewhere between the self-sufficiency that, if overdone, can make one an isolated person, seemingly friendless and indifferent to the need for friendship, and the dependent who cannot perform the simplest task without encouragement, there is a happy mean. None of us can afford the luxury of life without others who need us. Dr. Henry once put this statement of human needs most simply when he said that all of us need a job and a friend. All of us is a broad term that by no means excludes homosexuals. Perhaps theirs is a greater need than that of many others.

Certainly the homosexual, like any other mortal, will be happier with a rewarding job. It will be worth a great deal of effort on his part; and he may require all the help he can get to find it. Once having found it, he will be able, through his work, to make a valid contribution to the common life. Few of us are able to find the work that brings us the greatest happiness because we are genuinely useful. Most of us contrive to make something of the jobs that come to hand. It is a little difficult for us, if we are not disposed completely to renounce the world, to scrub floors for the glory of God. But, if need be, we can scrub them for a pay check.

Denied, through lack of wife and family, the satisfaction of home life, the homosexual must look more and more to his work to bring him what might in some sort compensate him for this deprivation. This is especially true as he grows older. The more satisfactory his work, the better able he is to face the world. In such a case, St. Augustine's motto, *laborare est orare,* can be liberally translated: the truest prayer is work. This may be a reason why some homosexuals, consciously or unconsciously, gravitate to professions that can give emotional satisfaction—teaching, social work, the ministry, and the like. To a considerable degree, some men are enabled in this wise to sublimate their sexual drives.

Many writers speak feelingly of the loneliness of the homosexual. As we consider this aspect of his war within himself, the need for work and a few good friends becomes increasingly understandable. Many a homosexual says that loneliness drives him out to the search for sexual companionship. This may be an oversimplification. There are those who think that it is only superficially that the search is conducted for physical intimacies. In 1938 we observed that it was the thrill of the chase, rather than the sex act itself that impelled men to seek sexual companionship.[8] Time has shown this observation to be in need of modification; it is true only in part.

It could well be that what is sought is perhaps less the pursuit, the conquest, or even the consummation, but relief from a devastating loneliness. This is highly conjectural, of course; but, as one observes the need of homosexuals to foregather with those who present little or no threat to their security, the conjecture is borne out to a very considerable degree. A wit once observed that the trouble with cliches was that they contained so much truth. How true is the one that tells us misery loves company. The need for friendship—tolerant, understanding friendship, an easy give-and-take relationship—is crying, especially for those who must make them serve as substitutes for home, wife and children. Among the younger men, friends are easily acquired and just as easily sent on their way. Sometimes a man is asked how many childhood friends he still has; how many friendships have lasted ten years; or five years. Even taking into account the ease with which Americans pull up stakes, the number of individuals with a host of acquaintances and few friends is much too large.

Recently a man who had to appear in court on a homosexual charge was instructed by his lawyer to produce what the law calls character witnesses. He was the holder of a position of some importance. Hence he was understandably timorous about bringing his professional colleagues to court to speak in his behalf. He cast around among the more presentable of his homosexual acquaintances in search of men whose appearance would not call attention to their sexual propensities. Those he asked to come to court had all sorts of business to occupy them elsewhere—they were so sorry. Perhaps it is necessary, the world being what it is, to make allowances for those who decided that their fears would not permit them to render this service to a friend in need. Yet the haste with which they seized upon any excuse to save their skins is an excellent illustration of what is meant by fair weather friends. The schoolboy's definition of a friend is one who knows the worst and is still willing to "stick around" has more than a little applicability. But schoolboys, it is said, need not consult their fears of guilt by association. That the homosexual needs genuine friends is obvious.

Here someone may say that what has been written has reference only to homosexuals without much character. That is true. There are those who have stood loyally by friends in their time of trouble, and who have gone to great lengths to deliver them from their peril, often at considerable risk to their own reputations. No one denies this for a moment; there are many such. It must be said again and again that there are homosexuals and homosexuals. This is as good a place as any to say unequivocally that there are homosexual citizens of exemplary character (save in so far as some would deny any sexually deviated person could be so described) who make substantial contributions to the common life. Homosexuals are people: all people have both good and evil qualities.

Existing as so many do, under conditions such as those endured by those who lived in fear of a domiciliary visit by the Gestapo, it is not at all difficult to see how fear would have an adverse effect on the psychological adjustment of homosexual men. The surprising thing is that, considering the obstacles society has placed before them, so many homosexuals have made so much of their lives. Here, of course, we speak in the most general terms. Objection has been raised to statements of this sort on the ground that the only homosexuals with whom a helping agency might have commerce are those who come to it in one or another form of trouble. We are asked to take into account the innumerable men of whom we have never heard and who are not likely to get into hot water. It goes without saying that an institution concerned with helping men out of trouble will not, save only inferentially, be able to supply very much in the way of direct evidence about those of whose lives it knows nothing. None the less, it is fairly safe to assume that, from an acquaintance with approximately five thousand men with whom The George W. Henry Foundation has been in touch during a quarter of a century, it knows something about at least the external phenomena of homosexuality. And it is blinking facts when men choose to deny the effect of social pressures on those who must live with their homosexuality. Those who can do so are incurable optimists.

As the homosexual reviews his situation, especially in times of crisis when guilt feelings become more troublesome, he can derive comfort from the fact that what he might consider his moral derelictions are not necessarily absolutes. As one Catholic confessor put it, it is seldom that one enters a situation he might subsequently regard as abhorrent with what is called the full consent of the will. It is highly doubtful that one becomes involved in a situation distinguished more for emotion than cerebration in the thought of consciously contravening the laws of Church and State. Such moral culpability as he may have is relative. His dilemma is not unlike that of St. Paul who spoke of a thorn in the flesh that impelled him to do that which he deplored. And, as he considers his guilts in his war within himself, the homosexual is duty bound to consider the social pressures that helped to create them, and the part these pressures play in his picture of himself. He can honestly reject the hasty, ill-considered, unscientific opinion that brands him a criminal and an outcast. There are too many homosexuals who are quick to accept the judgmental attitudes of society as an excuse for throwing up the sponge and admitting defeat. But is this necessary?

If he is willing to face the fact that there are handicaps to be overcome, and is willing to do his part to surmount them, the homosexual can, if he will, make a great deal of his life. Is his case too different from that of the man who is handicapped by economic deprivation? The number of Americans who have risen to commanding positions from homes of obscurity and poverty is legion. There are those who deny that this is possible in these latter days. It may be somewhat more difficult, but careers are still open to talent. It is all very well to say, for instance, that, although Al Smith rose to be a candidate for the Presidency from Oliver Street, there are millions who must remain in the slums. Not all of us can rise to such dazzling heights.

In many respects the homosexual is a handicapped person, even though there are those, as has been said, to whom this is a thought unpleasant to contemplate. There are many other groups in the same situation. The Negro has more to overcome than others of a different pigmentation. And the Jew has to get over a few more hurdles than those whose forebears were born into some other church. The fates have dealt unkindly with the homosexual; but other groups have found themselves entered in life's obstacle race. Some against whom the odds seemed heaviest have actually enjoyed the struggle, and, in the process, have done well for humanity as well as for themselves. Others have turned out to be what Dr. Robert Lindner called rebels without a cause. And still others have gone under. That is the way of the world. Whether it bespeaks the survival of the fittest, one does not profess to know. The gods are sometimes kind to those who are able to make use of the tools that come to hand.

The homosexual is not altogether helpless because of the handicaps under which he labors. There are many things he can do to help himself. He can take advantage of the circumstances in his situation that he is able to control. Sometimes he will need help clearly to discern these. Sometimes he will require aid to resolve conflicts that can be perceived intellectually, but before which he is powerless emotionally. Never is he permitted to forget that he is regarded as a stranger and a sojourner in a land where Church, State, and those who make them up have united to remind him of his equivocal position. Let there be no mistake about the matter. Resolving one's conflicts against these odds is no easy task. Some may be able to do so; others fall by the wayside. Though the price is great, the rewards are greater.

No matter how hard he may struggle, there are however, limits to what a man may be able to do for himself. As his situation is one not altogether of his own making, so, likewise, it is doubtful that he can extricate himself through his own unaided efforts. Much has to be done to change the view of the society that has helped to put him in his uncomfortable position. For a person in need of help, here and now, it is cold comfort to tell him that there is a better day coming. Is he altogether unlike the prisoner who is told by a well-meaning visitor that, if he endures his hardships manfully, he is making an excellent preparation for the time when he will be released? Today's homosexuals need help here and now.

Some gifted homosexual writer may feel moved to come forth with a book like the Apocalypses of Daniel and Revelation that would comfort his brethren in their time of "abuses and afflictions." No matter what its cause may be, the condition of every homosexual is such that he needs all the encouragement he can get. In the long run, society is poorer for what has been done to him. Sooner or later, in one form or another, it will have to pay the bill for what its rejection has cost in the way of contributions to the common weal that homosexuals were prevented from making.

When one of its parts become ill, the whole body suffers. When the physician is called to treat (let us say) an injured eye, he puts to rights what is wrong with it. By so doing, he restores the whole body to health. When some of its members are at war with each other, the whole body we call the community suffers. Therefore it would seem that society is under some obligation to seek ways and means to resolve the conflicts within those who compose it.

The health of the community depends upon its having useful and healthy citizens. The problems of those handicapped by their internal conflicts are therefore of concern to the social order. What it proposes to do about the matter remains to be seen. So long as it demands uniformity through the compulsion of its members to obey its rules, its government may be efficient enough. But there will always be the nonconformists who create problems through physical, or mental, or social incapacity, or through their tender consciences. And of these, many will be at war with themselves because they are torn between their duty to organized society and the need to follow the leading of their natures. Thus, once again, we are thrown into the conflict of interests between the one and the many, the individual and the group, the right of the citizen and the necessity of state. In all probability, the many appear to have somewhat the better of the argument. They can demand conformity and have the power to enforce their demand. And the few will suffer, in greater or less degree. That is the price men must pay for living in a society. But the good society, in its own interest, will see that its price is not too high.

Somewhere and somehow there is a compromise, a *via media,* to be found. We are engaged in its quest.

CHAPTER X

THE QUEST FOR GUIDING PRINCIPLES

> ...If each minority, each professional group, and each citizen would imagine himself in the other's shoes, everybody's rights would have firmer support. The beginning of justice is the capacity to generalize and make effective one's private sense of wrong, thus turning it to public account. The pursuit of justice is not the vain pursuit of a remote abstraction; it is a continuing direction for our daily conduct.
>
> —*Chief Justice Earl Warren*[1]

When The George W. Henry Foundation opened its doors to those who knocked, it began the little understood task of helping the sexually maladjusted to find ways of living acceptable to themselves and to society. Today a considerably different climate of opinion prevails with respect to the discussion of the problems of sexual deviation than when Dr. Henry began his researches. Chiefly the gain has been in the direction of frank and open discussion of the problem. No longer is it furtive and clandestine; nor is it confined to the places where scholars meet, remote from the affairs of ordinary men, to communicate with each other in their special language. The proverbial man in the street discovered that the problems of sexual behavior concerned him; therefore he proposed to talk about them. Some of the talk makes a great deal of sense; and some of it justifies the fears of the arch-conservatives that a little learning is a dangerous thing. Many changes in the public view of sexual variations have come about since the mid-nineteen-thirties. So far as one can see, the changes have been for the better.

There is a growing awareness that the community's attempt to cure social ills by the harsh treatment of those involved in sexual divergences has been less than successful. On every side we see evidences of a feeling that the laws attempting to regulate the sexual commerce of human beings are antiquated, and that punishments meted out to violators of these laws are out of keeping with the seriousness of the offenses they are designed to suppress. Their severity makes them a faulty instrument for the community to use to discourage behavior it cannot tolerate. Society has been learning the futility of punishment; as a preventive of crime or as a means or retribution it has gone by the board. However, as was pointed out, the same society that hopes to rehabilitate a forger or an arsonist has its misgivings when a homosexual becomes involved in the processes of criminal justice.

Many explanations have been offered for the slowness of society to abandon its punitive attitudes toward sexual deviates. Someone has facetiously pointed out that the homosexual is a two-fold menace to church and state. Because he does not marry and beget children to become cannon fodder, the State considers him a bad investment. Because he deprives the Church of potential souls to be saved through his failure to marry and breed children, he is a violator of the Biblical injuction to increase and multiply. Therefore he might be considered a heretic. At all events society has hitherto disposed of its sexual deviators, when they appeared before its bar of justice, by assigning to them the most rigorous and protracted of its punishments. Twenty year terms for sodomy are common in the penal laws; one or two states impose life terms. Even if judges and juries are hesitant to employ them, they are there to be used; and used occasionally they are Savage penalties here and the threat of hellfire hereafter have failed to eradicate the homosexual from the scene.

There are many theories extant why society undertakes, in the Anglo-Saxon world, to visit its sexual deviationists with such cruel symbols of its displeasure at what they do. The efforts of humanitarians to mitigate the severity of the law's punishments have extended to almost every other offense than the homosexual ones. Why is this so? For one thing, the average citizen has been conditioned to dislike homosexuals. The laws are enforced or quietly allowed to slumber as they receive the support of the people. Public prosecutors apparently feel that an outraged public opinion requires that the community make examples of those men who are charged with offenses of a homosexual nature that are considered violations of the public decencies. That has been the attitude for centuries.

Today we are beginning to realize that society is preparing to revise its views. Here a little and there a little, we see unmistakable signs that the public is not so certain that the homosexual is so great a threat to its security as had been hitherto supposed. And the wealth of scientific data on the causes and conditions of homosexual activity and interest is being shared by those in the higher intellectual reaches with those whose opinions they hope ultimately to influence. The public is beginning to take the trouble to inform itself about what is involved. It is beginning to suspect what may have been felt for a long time: the opinions that go the rounds are a hodge-podge of prejudice, half-truth and irresponsible conjecture. In the past, the world looked for guidance to the moralists and doctors of the church. Perhaps these men did as well as they could with the information they had at their disposal. But new light has been thrown on the subject of the sexual deviations, and the means whereby men gratify needs considered abnormal. In this light, men have begun seriously to question the wisdom of some fundamental assumptions hitherto regarded as sacrosanct. They are turning for guidance to those whose professional competence requires that they present facts rather than opinions.

The psychiatrist, in his work with the individuals he treated, discovered that the problem was a social one: the patient dos not live in a vacuum. It is necessary that we keep prominently in our thinking the ineluctable fact that the homosexual lives in society. In larger part, his difficulties arise out of his inability to meet the demands it makes on him. The problem of homosexuality, therefore, is as much that of the body social as it is of the individual. It seems obvious, then, that society should set about discovering an effective method to deal with it. Thus far its efforts in that direction can be summed up in one word—repression.

Is the sexual behavior of the citizen properly the subject of regulation by law? Those of a traditional turn of mind would say that this is a matter of divine ordinance, and therefore not to be questioned by man. The Biblical rules prescribed the most painful consequences for those who violated the sexual taboos. They also provided the most severe penalties for a great variety of criminal offenses, some of which found their way into the penal code of an American commonwealth that was copied in part from the Book of Leviticus. But men found it expedient to abrogate what is now considered barbaric penal legislation—except for the homosexual offenses. Vestiges of Mosaic pronouncements of the will of a god of vengeance are still to be found in our statutes that seek to wipe out homosexual intercourse.

In the Declaration of Independence, we are told that "Governments are instituted among men, deriving their just powers from the consent of the governed." The operative words are *the consent of the governed.* Do we have certain knowledge that our laws dealing with sexual irregularities express the moral standards of the people at this time? Do our sexual laws accomplish this? The Preamble of the Constitution of the United States is specific in stating that one of its objects is to promote the general welfare. Do our repressive social laws with regard to sexual irregularity do this? Thomas Aquinas calls law "a

rule of reason for the purpose of the common good.'"³ Many serious
and responsible students question whether it is posible to advance the
common good through an attempt to regulate what might well be
considered a matter of private morality.

Laws become obsolete or unworkable, and they are quietly permitted
to lapse into innoucuous desuetude. Or their abuse becomes so flag-
rant that public opinion forces their repeal. Certainly the framers
of the ill-fated Prohibition Amendment considered that they were
laying down a "rule of reason for the purpose of the common good."
Little did they anticipate the abuses that made its enforcement a
carnival of crime. Never for a moment did they foresee the unholy
alliance of criminals and fanatics to bring the administration of
public law into disrepute. The descendants of the gangsters spawned
by the "noble experiment" have yet to be eliminated from the American scene. The Prohibition Law had to be repealed because it undertook to legislate on a matter of private morality. Is our sexual behavior a matter of private concern or one of public morals?

There was a time when adultery was a crime on the statute books.
It is a dead letter today. A public prosecutor asking for an indictment
for adultery would have a hard time with even the most unsophisticated Grand Jury. Laws that have outlived their usefulness are allowed
to lapse when they are discovered to be unenforceable. Even statutes
that undertake to suppress homosexual intercourse (and these have
considerable public support) are not too vigorously enforced so far
as attempts to ferret out illicit relations of men of full age, conducted
in private, are concerned. At least they do not exercise the vigilance of
the police in sophisticated metropolitan communities. What is done
in the country is another matter. One may assume that, by and large,
in the cities, few prosecutions are undertaken for the private sexual
intercourse of two males. But the laws remain on the statute books;
and there is always the danger that someone with an axe to grind
might organize a witch hunt and wipe off the dust that has been
accumulating on the code books.

No method has yet been devised of taking a plebiscite to determine
what sexual laws meet the general approval of the voters, or whether
the people feel that there is need for revision. Every once in a while
someone quotes Mister Dooley's dictum that the Supreme Court
follows the election returns. Public officials, especially those who
want to be re-elected, have a very keen ear for what the people want.
Citizens with a concern for reform of the laws regulating the homosexual offenses would do well to see that what Bagehot called the

felt need for these changes is kept before the notice of the men who look to the common suffrage to hold their jobs. How this may be done is not a matter within the competence of this book. There are men who make an excellent living at influencing public opinion and helping get laws passed. They have their uses.

There seems only the most casual interest at this time on the part of the public in demanding reconsideration of the social laws with respect to sexual offenses. For the most part there is a disposition to let well enough alone. When some shocking sex crime is spread over the sensational newspapers, there is apt to be a clamor for stricter enforcement and more drastic punishments. When that subsides, a general apathy prevails. Those who advocate change are regarded as voices crying in the wilderness, to whom very little attention is paid. That is why, as Dr. Henry says, society as a whole "must be educated and kept informed so it may deal with the problem effectively."[4] Until the whole community becomes convinced that there is something seriously amiss in our method of dealing with sexual deviates, little can be expected. It would seem, therefore, that public education to the need for change is prerequisite for penal reform.

How shall we go about this? There is little doubt that accurate information should be at our command and widely disseminated. We are required to examine critically the postulates upon which our present laws are based, and even go behind them, to ascertain the factors that made the legislation seem desirable. In many cases, our criminal codes came to us from the church in its attempts to regulate conduct it deemed sinful. Scholars have devoted a great deal of study to the interrelatedness of ecclesiastical and secular law. And there are still places where the bill of divorcement between the civil and the canon law has not been too widely published. There is no doubt of the influence of the church's thought on the common law. But it is important to make a very clear distinction between what the church considers sin and the public law determines to be criminal. Probably the essence of crime is that its harmful effects go beyond the person of the criminal. Yet even that has some limitations. There was a time when the state legislated against attempts on the part of the individual to take his life. It still punishes certain attempts to harm oneself. For instance, the laws against the possession of narcotic drugs were conceived to prevent human beings from becoming slaves to an evil addiction. The practicality of the law, as those who work among young addicts testify, remains still to be seen. Yet, by and large, crimes to be crimes must be committed against the person or the property of another.

With the exception of attempted *felo de se*,' (and nowadays most places send for the doctor, rather than the policeman to deal with would-be suicides) the imagination is taxed when asked to supply the elements of a crime that one can commit in his solitariness. Even what the Japanese penalized as the crime of possessing dangerous thoughts necessitated a certain amount of publication of the thoughts for them to become dangerous. The church has no such problem with respect to sin. Sin can be committed by thought and word, as well as by deed. And we are told in the Scriptures that the contemplation of adultery, for instance, is every bit as bad as engaging in an adulterous act. A man sins against himself, his neighbor, or his God. There must be another with (or against) whom he sins before the sin becomes a crime. That one sins *with* another in the eyes of the church, when a homosexual act is committed, is undeniable. Whether he commits a crime *against* his neighbor permits a somewhat wider latitude of interpretation.

The law's attitude toward the whole subject of sexual irregularities has been strongly influenced by ecclesiastical prepossessions about sin. That seems obvious. Equally obvious is the fact that the church's emphasis on the expiation of sin was carried over into the state's demand for the punishment of crime. As the church visited ecclesiastical pains and penalties on the sinner, so the state awarded civil penalties to the criminal. The church endeavored to root out what it considered undesirable manifestations of the bodily appetites: these would detract from the moral perfection required for entrance into the Kingdom of Heaven. The state joined with the church in visiting carnal iniquities with bodily suffering. Thus, in many men's minds, sin and crime were equated.

Here is how an Englishman views the process:

"The desire for food and the desire for procreation seemed to be the strongest of the desires of the body; if these could be defeated then release was possible. So the idealists set about to defeat sex. They established a standard of complete abstinence—the only logical standard if it be granted that the body and its desires are peculiarly a part 'of this world.' Complete abstinence, of course, was not possible for everyone; but nevertheless sex relations were carnal, of the flesh, and the flesh was a part of the shadow. Since the complete ideal could not be attained by the ordinary man the nearest approach to it should be the rule. Sex should be used for the 'creation of souls' and

for no other purpose; any other use than this and any other intention
was sinful. This standard created an asceticism of sorts for most
labourers—very few men could enter into the full rigours of the ideal;
yet it was asceticism, and it was an effort to 'defeat the body.'

"Here, then, was the general Christian ethical standard of the past
derived from a Christian belief in Eternity and a life in Time, and
from the assumption that the life in Time was necessarily lower, or
less real, than the other. The standard worked. It explained to men
the function of labour, always a very difficult function for the mass
of men to fit in with an intelligent universe; and it explained and made
purposeful the function of sex. In a sense, under this standard, the
body ceased to be a shadow, that was the great Christian accomplish-
ment of the past. In spite of the fact that the body was regarded as
less real than 'spirit' it became linked with purpose; its appetites
were linked with ideas, and consequently men did find a fulfilment
of life purpose under this standard; they knew what they were about.
There could be deviation from the standard, but the deviation was
wrong; it was sinful; it made more difficult the entrance of the deviator into the true light of 'the other world.'

"By and large this is still the official judgment of Christian Church
upon work and sex relationships today.

"But modern standards commending themselves as good to the majority of men, most of whom call themselves Christians, have largely
destroyed this Christian ethic and consequently taken its purpose from
it. The destruction of the standard means the destruction of the
specifically Christian structure—quite apart from the other influences
of the modern world all bearing in the same direction. It is not a case
of whether the traditional Christian ethic is right or wrong; under
modern conditions it is seen to be impracticable, and thus it is tacitly
ignored."⁶

The church's concern for the regulation of bodily appetites was incorporated into the social laws. This was done when church and state
shared a common ethical ideal, that at one time may have been universally accepted. That ideal, in the light of twenty centuries of
Christian experience, could be regarded as difficult, if not impossible,
of attainment. Is it not time, then, to set out to examine its fundamental assumptions?

To the traditionalist it is unthinkable to question a standard of conduct that is considered to be of divine origin. Nevertheless, evidence
is constantly accumulating, pointing conclusively to the fact that the
assumption in itself no longer meets the need for an authoritative

statement of what constitutes approved sexual conduct that the people as a whole are able to respect and follow. If it is unlawful for men to experiment sexually in ways that fail to meet the approval of the guardians of tradition, then they feel that they have some right to know the reasons for the prohibitions.

Doubtless there are many to whom this presumption to question authority will be highly repugnant. Their solution is that society tighten its belt and impose even severer penalties on men who act as though the sexual regulations fail to serve a useful purpose. What this will accomplish is open to question. It has been tried time out of mind—never with any conspicuously successful results. Human behavior cannot be completely controlled by edict. Yet society has employed, and continues to employ, the twin clubs of judgment and condemnation. For the most part, the injunction: "Judge not, that ye be not judged; condemn not, lest ye be condemned" has been ignored.

We have been considering the situation of the homosexual chiefly in the light of the judgment and condemnation society has visited upon him. We have tried to show that his position is derived from emotion and preconceived opinion, rather than in reason. On every side, there is evidence of the evil that prejudice can do. And there is little to show that society has made many strenuous efforts to overcome it. Sometimes we see signs that permit us to hope that we have made a start in this direction. Have we?

So far as can be seen, the prejudices that govern the social attitudes in respect to men's sexual behavior still persist. But the social order makes only sporadic efforts to enforce the dictates based on its prejudices. Occasionally we are required to pull the forelock in a gesture of obeisance to the official standards, as, during the French Enlightenment, prominent freethinkers were given an unconsecrated wafer at Mass, so that the conventions would be satisfied when one who seemed important could be seen outwardly observing the forms of the state religion. When it comes to what we actually do about the matter, we proceed without paying too much attention to the standards to which we render lip service. Who set them? Do they commend themselves to all men in our culture as the only way for people to behave sexually? If so, why are they so generally ignored?

Certainly no one can supply us with answers to these questions that will satisfy everyone. Nor is he who propounds the questions altogether sure that he asks the right ones. Certainly there is a great difference between ideal and performance. And it is evident that the sins of the flesh, especially in their less orthodox forms, give society a great deal more trouble than other acts that are deemed immoral.

There are scarcely any who would question the right of the community to make rules for the better ordering of its corporate life. The social compact lays the duty upon the state to preserve the public order. Without rules of some sort, any social structure would fall apart. The minute two people live together, there must be a certain minimum of convention—preferably reached by mutual agreement—to avoid friction. When any relation goes beyond what a person does in his solitariness, the society in which he lives has a stake in what he does. Otherwise, the life of man as Hobbes says in the *Leviathan,* would be "solitary, poor, nasty, brutish, and short."

If we assume, as many responsible persons do, that the laws that seek to repress homosexual activity are ill-considered, this does not mean that they are all to be abrogated. A certain amount of regulation will always be necessary to keep in order those to whom the *argumentum ad baculum* is the only one they can respect. Compromises will have to be made on both sides. It is possible, even probable, that the private consenting homosexual intercourse of two adult persons will be stricken from the list of punishable offenses. But there are fringe offenses that will still need to be dealt with summarily. Society cannot afford to relinquish control over any sort of behavior that is patently unsuitable. Strong measures must be held in reserve to be used against those who offend against adolescents and children. Doubtless the social order will find some form of coercion necessary to be used in the cases of those who make nuisances of themselves by importuning in public places. Very few would be willing to have society relinquish the protection of the young or be without the power to discipline those who abuse places for the convenience or enjoyment of all citizens.

Important though it may be, legislative reform is only a step toward relieving the homosexual of impediments to full citizenship. It is a much-needed step, to be sure, and a step long overdue. But just as man cannot be made good by Act of Parliament, so the homosexual's position will be improved only in part through the removal by law of some of his penal disabilities. Much more is required than the cancellation of a law an English judge called the Blackmailers' Charter.' The Supreme Court opened the doors of Southern public schools to Negro children, confirming them in their legal rights. Much more has yet to be done to create an atmosphere that invests the Negro with the full dignity that is rightfully his. So is it with the sexual deviate. Even though the law will, sooner or later, free him of some of his present-day criminal liability, it will take a long time before he is regarded as a free man in a free society.

How go about the business of educating men to their responsibilities and duties to their homosexual brethren? At the moment, we are in somewhat the same position as the judge who admonishes the members of the jury to leave their prejudices behind them as they file into the place where they will consider their verdict. The judge has a right to hope that the jury will, by some magic, forget their prejudices. The community is the jury of public opinion by whom the homosexual hopes to be judged with something approaching objectivity. Perhaps this is possible today. But it is not easy, even with the best will in the world, for the community to divest itself of its inherited antipathy toward individuals whose sexual needs fail to follow conventional patterns. More share this view than the ignorant and those who make up what used to be called the lower orders.

A judge of a criminal court had a friend visiting him. After lunch he left his friend in his chambers while he tried a troublesome case. When the trial was over, and the judge was shuffling his papers preparatory to sentencing the morning's crop of petty offenders, he sent an officer to summon his visitor. His instructions to the bailiff, given in a tone of voice that could be heard several feet away, were: "Tell Mister So-and-So to come in; I'm going to sentence the "fairies."

The attitude of this judge, in many respects a faithful and conscientious public servant, is not too dissimilar to that of many of his fellow-citizens who profess a certain amount of enlightenment. That it will be difficult to modify attitudes such as these must be obvious to all save the most impractical souls to whom the wish is father to the thought. Not only must we change an attitude to be found in the Pharisee, the moralizer, the self-righteous; but we must also upset the apple cart called the line of least resistance. It is hard to go against ingrained views that have been unquestioned for centuries. There is little likelihood that the cause of the homosexual will be a particularly popular one; and those who espouse it would be well-advised to bear in mind that there is always the chance they may be regarded with a certain amount of suspicion. One need only to look at the example in the Introduction to this book to see how proper Bostonians regarded William Lloyd Garrison when he took to agitating for the emancipation of men and women held in slavery.

Condemnation is easy; equally easy is the policy of the ostrich. It is not at all difficult to hide one's head in the sand. Or one can do less than that: it is always possible simply to look the other way. That is how the priest and the levite in the parable of the Good Samaritan chose to sidestep a difficult problem. Polite society has managed to act as though there were no problem of homosexuality to concern it. When someone was unfortunate enough to get into trouble, he was quietly locked up in prison, and everyone called it a day. Yet the problem has been with us since man first began to write history—perhaps even before that. Thus far no one has found a satisfactory solution; we continue in the old ways of repression. A measure of penal reform is within the bounds of possibility, even of probability. That at least is a start. Can society afford to admit that here is a problem for which there is no solution in sight?

In our search for a workable solution that would be generally acceptable, it is necessary that we acquire more knowledge of why men behave as they do. The more we learn the more we are able to pass along to others. Thus there is a chance for accurate information to spread downward and outward. Man has a way of aping his betters, or those he considers his betters. No opinion, no matter how disreputable, will be long without supporters if enough of the great ones of the earth can be found to endorse it. Over the doors of the New York Public Library are carved the words: "Ye shall know the truth, and the truth shall make you free." But, as Pontius Pilate sadly inquired, "What is truth?"

Those who subscribe to the shoddiest notions about the ways and works of sexual deviators feel that their supply of misinformation is quite true. They fail to trouble themselves to inquire whence came the opinions that pass for fact. It is a great deal easier to hug a moth-eaten myth to one's breast than to investigate its veracity. But, as one is tempted to go on in this strain, it must be remembered that a myth is a primitive way of explaining what is not altogether clear. Behind most myths lies a substratum of truth. What is there to the myth about the homosexual? Perhaps this. Somehow homosexuals are not as other men are. And, when we recall Zangwill's definition of prejudice as dislike of the unlike, the matter becomes much more understandable. Homosexuals are different; therefore they are bad; therefore they are . . .

How much of a threat to the social order does the homosexual actually offer? It is probable that he gives no more or no less discomfort than any other sort of nonconformist. Feeling can be, and is, much more uncompromising against the homosexual than it might be against some other minorities; but this statement is subject to quite a bit of qualification, there being so many variables involved. When occasion demands, it is possible to work up a community to fever heat over the derelictions of almost any minority group. This has been done before, and it will, alas, be done many times more. So, we ask, if the homosexual does threaten the community's security, (and of this there is no evidence that a law court would accept without a great deal of qualification) wherein does the threat lie? In what way does he do real, or even potential, harm? If he does, are we not under some obligation to ask ourselves whether society itself is not at least partly accountable, and therefore obligated, in its own protection, to repair what might be the damage he does? But it has not yet been demonstrated that the homosexual is *ipso facto* a threat to anyone; his offenses are something else again. Shall we take a firm hand against all ready-to-wear clothing salesmen because someone who works in a dishonest establishment sells shoddy merchandise? If, in the course of centuries of ill treatment, homosexuals occasionally turn up with some unpleasant characteristics, must not society ask itself how these things came to be? And is it right in condemning all for the sins of the few? Again and again it must be repeated that we are required to adequately inform ourselves about what is actually involved. It is self evident that it is too easy to confuse terms and facts. This we all do. Only by accurate information are we enabled to judge what is involved in a problem about which many pontificate but few have knowledge.

As a matter of fact, scientific inquiry has brought relatively little to light about what lies behind the external manifestations of the phenomena we call the sexual deviations. There is no-man's land to be explored and charted. It is true that a number of "educated guesses" have been made as to their causes. Common factors regularly appear in the cases of large numbers of individuals; but whether, and to what extent, these common factors can be regarded as causative is something about which we know next to nothing, comparatively speaking. Again and again, competent scholars have observed that we have only begun to scratch the surface of the problem.

While the scientific workers seek to uncover the roots of the problem, and devote themselves to the quest for cause and possible cure, troubled men still require help in times of crisis. No one would think of asking that the devastating effects of an arrest or the threats and menaces of a blackmailer be postponed until science was able to disclose the whole problem in all of its ramifications and give full directions for its solution. Simply to suggest this is sufficient. Medicine knows nothing like what it needs to know about cancer: those who suffer from it are given everything our present knowledge makes available. The doctors do their best with the tools they have. So, when one needs to be helped through a crisis that stems from his sexual maladjustment, those with knowledge and access to sources of help must do their best for him with what equipment they have or can procure. Steps to guide him to places where assistance to prevent the recurrence of crises may be suggested; but certainly to tell a man in his time of adversity that he can have help only if he will do what we think good for him smacks of dubious ethics. There are, of course, those who question the wisdom of treating a symptom and hoping that the disease will somehow take care of itself. But that does not dispose of the matter of what to do when an emergency arises, requiring action then and there.

Those in a position to make that sort of immediate help available would do well to consider its implications in relation to what needs to be done over a long period of time. We need to think of the possibilities of taking preventive measures to help one who lives from crisis to crisis—and there are too many such among the sexually maladjusted. This presupposes that those engaged in works of help-fulness should have a unifying philosophy to enable them to view a situation not only in the terms of the requirements of the immediate dire circumstances but also how to utilize a catastrophic experience as a means of education to the possibilities of less harrowing ways of achieving one's sexual satisfactions. To do this effectively, it is needful to set up a workable *terminus ad quem.* Surely the *terminus a quo,* the starting point, is a man's need. And the need of which we speak is to be found in his view thereof. It may be discovered that what an individual thinks he needs and his real need are not quite the same. But there is the place where we must start—from the occasion that moves him to come for help. It is said that every man is, in some sort, a philosopher. Should not a philosophy of helping people out of trouble be as much the concern of the therapist and those he helps as the social and moral philosopher? Probably those engaged in practical day-to-day works of helpfulness live their philos-ophies: they leave it to others to formulate them.

We begin with the consideration of how best to reconcile one's opinion of the legitimacy of his needs with that held by the social order in which he operates. In the case of our undertaking to work out the beginnings of a philosophy that will enable us to deal with the sexual deviations, it may well be that we are trying to find a formula in Hegelian terms. The *thesis* is an enlightened view of the homosexual's place in the social order; the *antithesis* is the present repressive view of the community; we seek the *synthesis*. What principles should guide us in our search? And how relate these principles to our theories of society as a whole? Certainly the problem of homosexuality does not exist in part of our minds, isolated from the contemplation of all other aspects of human nature and conduct. Likewise, it must be borne in mind that principles are universal; in their application they tend to address themselves to the particular. This is one of the dangers inherent in the making of moral codes. We get into trouble when we try to fit ideals into a Procrustean bed of legislation. We are helped in our thinking on this point by Professor Bryn-Jones: "The test of a moral code in any generation is not its measure of perfection, because perfection is hard to seek, but whether it constitutes an advance, however small, to perfection. The ideal is a standard of judgment, a criterion of quality, and our judgments based on it must always be relative."[8]

In seeking ideals of sexual behavior that commend themselves as binding upon the public conscience, society must distinguish between the concept of the good life it currently upholds and the good itself. It must be doubly careful when it sets up a standard to be enforced through the application of legal sanctions. All the law can do is to proscribe conduct it is certain the community will not tolerate. Here is the dilemma of the idealist. Here is what is meant by saying that a man can not be made good by Act of Parliament. The conduct the law requires of a citizen might represent an ethical minimum—a compromise between the highest ethical demands a man may make upon himself and freedom to do as he pleases. The result may turn out highly satisfactory to the average citizen; his thinking may leave something to be desired, but his instincts are apt to be fairly sound.

We are prone to fall into the error of presuming that the ideals we espouse are obligatory upon all mankind. This is what Mr. Justice Holmes had in mind when he pointed out the impossibility of compelling the people of Louisiana to accept the civilization of Massachusetts. Here in essence is what is called ethical relativity.

There is evolution in the field of ethics as well as in biology. Hence we must take into account the evolution of our ideas of sexual morality. It is said that human nature cannot be changed; but the interpretation of is manifestations changes from generation to generation and from place to place. Here we are concerned to see if the standards appropriate to our modern society may be restated in the light of our present-day knowledge, and how best they may be made to serve our present-day needs.

As we review the place of the homosexual in the social order, and, as we seek the principles to guide us to lay the groundwork for its clarification in view of the contributions of the behavioral sciences, it would seem that our task is two-fold. We are called upon to take the steps that seem necessary to relieve him of most, if not all, of the burden that should never have been his. It is high time to consider the maleficent effect upon the whole social order of what happens when those who are part thereof, even though a very small part, must daily live with lack of understanding, prejudice, scorn, and sometimes even downright cruelty. There are signs that the burden may be lightened somewhat in the forseeable future. That is as it should be. But much more must be done before the commonplaces of informed circles become part and parcel of the opinions of everyman. How this is to be accomplished is something for all to ponder who are interested in seeing that the homosexual gets what Dr. Bailey calls simple justice. This is the first part of our task.

And the second part grows out of it naturally. We are called upon to lay the foundations of a philosophy to guide us as we do the practical things that are suggested here. This we may not do hurriedly. All that seems possible at this time is to suggest in broadest outline what is required. Nor need we expect immediate, whole-hearted acceptance of the fact that it is necessary to make changes in what men think proper ways to deal with their homosexual brethren. Professor Bryn-Jones calls us to a lively sense of the possible when he says: "There is no uniformity in the moral achievements of nations and peoples, and always, even among the most advanced, aspirations have to contend with the passions which in human nature are intertwined with man's nobler parts. These are the facts that determine the tempo of humanity's march."⁹

It is essential that society be kept reminded that all is not well with its treatment of those who fail to conform to the social laws and moral codes that regulate the sexual behavior of men. We are beginning to see signs of a growing awareness of the need for turning away from repression and coercion as a means to secure obedience to the dictates of the social order. Reason rather than force, in the view of an increasing number of responsible makers and leaders of opinion, should be the ultimate seat of authority.

Reason suggests that, so far as the sexual deviations are concerned, we should re-examine not a morality, but a view of morality, that may have outlived its usefulness. Are we not under a clear duty to inquire whether rules that may have served another age still have validity? Do they lighten the darkness of to-day's moral confusion? If they do not, where shall we turn for guidance in revising them? How shall we look for the road that leads to the heart of the matter?

Lack of imagination, apathy, and unquestioning obedience to a seemingly impregnable tradition have marked the history of man's attempts to deal with this persistent and perplexing problem of human nature and conduct. It follows that we would do well to look for answers that consider the legitimate need of the individual, and, at the same time, safeguard public order. Some of the answers may be found in the book of science. Some, but not all of them.

Those who see a failure of the social conscience in the way men treat their brethren who, "by reason of their sexual maladjustment are in trouble with themselves, the law, or society," [10] have heard a call to embark upon an intellectual and moral adventure. Some, actuated by religious motives, will seek reconsideration of the churches' positions with respect to the problem. Others may be concerned with unresolved conflicts of science, of the law, or of ethics. Still others view the homosexual as an example of man's inhumanity to man. The equivocal position of the sexual nonconformist troubles many who feel that he is deprived of the dignity with which men bear the burdens and share the blessings of a democratic society.

Where shall we begin our quest? How shall we set about the task of making freemen of those who feel themselves strangers in our midst. deprived of full citizenship? Justice Holmes points the way for us: "When men have realized that time has upset many fighting faiths, they may come to believe that the ultimate good is better reached by free trade in ideas—that the best test of truth is the power of the thought to get itself accepted in the competition of the market." [11] Centuries upon centuries ago one of the unknown writers of the Apocrypha counselled: "Mighty is the truth and it will prevail!" [12]

NOTES

CHAPTER I

1. From *The Life of the Spirit.* New York: Dodd, Mead & Co., 1899.

2. Thus it was, and thus, with some modifications and mitigations, it still is. But the official priesthood did not always have an easy time of it. Prophets rose from time to time to trouble the peace of Israel, and the prophets were never keen about making themselves friends of the Mammon who sits in high places. It might not be an altogether unprofitable exercise to recall that the prophet Nathan's disapproval of King David's philandering was quite vocal. (Vid. II Sam. xii.)

3. George W. Henry. *Sex Variants.* Two volumes, New York: Harper & Bro., 1941. One volume edition, *id.*, 1948.

4. George W. Henry. *All the Sexes.* New York: Rinehart & Co., 1955.

5. Philadelphia: W. B. Saunders Co., 1948.

6. Genesis i:27.

7. C. S. Lewis. *Surprised by Joy.* New York: Harcourt, Brace & Co., 1956.

8. Allen Drury. *Advise and Consent.* Garden City, New York: Doubleday & Co., 1959.

9. C. S. Lewis. *Op. cit.*

10. D. S. Bailey. *Homosexuality and the Western Christian Tradition.* New York: Longmans, Green & Co., 1955.

CHAPTER II

1. It is possible to say that the hoodlum homosexual, because of the greater accessibility of men, can be presumed to make increasing use of them as sex objects. As he becomes more and more accustomed to the conditions of life as a male prostitute, it is likewise to be presumed that his interest in women will lessen. A habit, or behavior pattern, can thus be seen in the process of formation. It is not too different from Pavlov's little dogs, who took to salivating when they heard the bell ring. There seems to be a good chance that, after a year or two of prostitution, his interests will be directed more and more toward the place where sex is obtainable with a minimum of effort. Whether his need for women will atrophy one does not profess to know. Furthermore statements made by male prostitutes are in need of being taken with many grains of salt. Usually men of this type, as has been suggested, boast of their enacting the so-called male role with their patrons. Sometimes what actually transpires is discovered to be quite at variance with what is reported. It is a belief commonly entertained about themselves by men of this ilk that, so long as one is the "man" at acts of homosexual intercourse, he is not a homosexual. The male prostitute is said to derive considerable comfort from this way of maintaining what he holds out his virility.

2. Henry and Gross. "Social Factors in the Case Histories of One Hundred Underprivileged Homosexuals," *Mental Hygiene,* October, 1938.

3. D. S. Bailey. *Op. cit.*

4. In an early paper ("Social Factors in the Case Histories of 100 Underprivileged Homosexuals," *Mental Hygiene,* Oct., 1938) Henry and Gross examined the social

implications of homosexuality, and set up what we considered a workable classification of social categories—orderly, hoodlum, fairy. The two men whose cases were mentioned in the beginning of this chapter, the young executive and the teacher, and the author of this autobiographical fragment, could be considered as representing the orderly homosexuals. Harry, the "hustler" constitutes a fair example of the group of hoodlum homosexuals, or male prostitutes. It is a work of supererogation further to consider the fairy in this place.

5. The reader is warned that this is a matter of opinion. The Early Church certainly had some very strong notions about those who engaged overtly in homosexual practices. They were not looked upon with much tolerance—certainly with no approval. Paul expressed himself quite forcibly about that particular set of sins of the flesh. His views are discussed in Dr. Bailey's *Homosexuality and the Western Christian Tradition* at some length. Turning to another analogy of the homosexual to members of minorities, consider him in relation to Jews. More than twenty years ago, the Foundation was consulted by a psychiatrist in charge of a study of sex offenders in a midwestern prison. We had been writing back and forth amicably until a suggestion was put out by this writer that there were certain similarities to be observed in society's treatment of homosexuals and members of other minorities— Jews, for instance. Back came an indignant letter: "Jews are good citizens; homosexuals are criminals." And this from a psychiatrist! When dealing with what might threaten the security of those who (Lord knows!) have enough to contend with, it is well to wear a rhinoceros hide.

6. Elie A. Cohen. *Human Behavior in a Concentration Camp.* New York: W. W. Norton & Co., 1953.

7. Cohen. *Id.*

Chapter III

1. From *Representative Government.* In Oakeshott: *Social and Political Documents of Contemporary Europe.* Cambridge (England): Cambridge University Press, 1939.

2. J. E. E. Dalberg-Acton (First Baron Acton): *Lectures on the French Revolution.* New York: Noonday Press, 1959.

3. Henry and Gross. *The Sex Offender: A Consideration of Therapeutic Principles.* Yearbook, National Probation Association, 1940. Reprinted by the Association as a pamphlet.

4. Henry and Gross. *Social Factors in the Case Histories of One Hundred Underprivileged Homosexuals. Supra.* All of these fears are based on the homosexual's knowledge of what he can expect at the hands of a rejecting society. As we suggest in Chapter X, an English judge called the English law under which homosexual acts are punished the Blackmailers' Charter.

5. George W. Henry. "Pastoral Counselling for Homosexuals," *Pastoral Psychology,* November, 1951.

6. Bailey, *op. cit.*

7. Peter Wildeblood. *A Way of Life.* London: Weidenfeld & Nicolson, 1956.

8. In his novel *Coningsby.*

9. Wildeblood. *Op. cit.*

10. I Thess. v: 21

CHAPTER IV

1. *De Anima,* Book I, Chapter 1,

2. More than thirty years ago, at a lecture attended by the author of this book, Harry Elmer Barnes said something like this: "There ·was a time when theology proudly called itself the queen of the sciences. Now mental hygiene has come to dispute her crown." There are many who continue to fight the battle between theology and science. Some even believe that the human mind is capable of division into water-tight compartments.

3. It is probably an ideal doctor-patient relationship that is being considered here. A psychiatrist with strong prejudices against homosexuals is well advised to ask himself whether the long association in the treatment process might do both doctor and patient more harm than good. There is much more likelihood of an ethical psychiatrist sending a patient elsewhere if his illness is such that the doctor has strong feelings against those who suffer from it.

4. A. A. Gross. "The Manners and Morals of Adjustment", *Mental Hygiene,* July 1939.

5. Psalms xxxvii: 25.

6. Peter Wildeblood. *Against the Law.* London: Weidenfeld & Nicolson, 1955. (American ed., New York: Julian Messner, 1959.)

7. Reservations by Dr. Curran and Dr. Whitby in the Wolfenden Report, viz: Sir J. Wolfenden, et al. *Report of the Committee on Homosexual Offenses and Prostitution.* Cmnd. 274. London: H. M. Stationery Office, 1957.

8. It may be taken for granted that the individual who is satisfied with his sexual way of life will not be interested in seriously investigating the possibilities of this sort of professional consultation.

9. Attention is called to the dissertation by Dr. William Wolfson, now Chief Psychologist of the State Hospital at Middletown, New York, in fulfillment of his requirements to become a master of arts at the City College of New York. In 1947, while a probation officer in one of New York's municipal criminal courts, he compared the condition of 100 men directed to take treatment with that of a similar number who went without help. The men treated, either by doctors or clergymen, did much better than those without professional help. Many more men were rearrested for similar offenses from the untreated group than was the case of those who were treated. Coercion was frankly employed, in the first instance, to get the men under treatment.

CHAPTER V

1. John H. C. Wu. *Fountain of Justice.* New York: Sheed & Ward, 1955.

2. *Ibid.*

3. *Ibid.*

4. Bailey, *op. cit.,*

5. New York: Prentice Hall, 1951.

6. Bailey, *op. cit.*

7. Rom. vii: 7.

8. *Novellae* for A. D. 536.

9. Oliver Wendell Holmes. *Collected Legal Papers.* New York: Harcourt, Brace & Co., 1920.

10. Sir J. Wolfenden, et al. *Supra.*

11. *Ibid.*

12. Sir W. Blackstone. *Commentaries on the English Law.*

13. From the Prayer for the Whole State of Christ's Church in the Communion Service of the (American) Protestant Episcopal Church. *Book of Common Prayer*, p. 74.

14. From an address at Princeton, quoted in Raymond B. Fosdick, *Chronicle of a Generation.* New York: Harper & Bro., 1958.

15. Felix Frankfurter. *Of Laws and Men.* New York: Harcourt, Brace & Co., 1956.

16. Sir J. Wolfenden, et al. *Supra.*

CHAPTER VI

1. C. Kilmer Myers. *Light the Dark Streets.* Greenwich, Conn.: Seabury Press, 1950.

2. Margaret Mead. *Male and Female.* New York: William Morrow & Co., 1949.

3. Mead, *op., cit.*

4. In the foreword to Henry: *All the Sexes, supra.*

5. Wildeblood: *A Way of Life, supra.*

6. *Ibid.*

7. From *Guilt.* New York: Sheed & Ward, 1952.

CHAPTER VII

1. From *An Historian's Approach to Religion.* London, New York, Toronto: Oxford University Press, 1956.

2. From the Foreword to Henry: *All the Sexes. Supra.*

3. George W. Henry. "Pastoral Counselling for Homosexuals," *Pastoral Psychology*, November, 1951.

4. In the foreword of the English edition of D. J. West. *The Other Man.* American edition published by William Morrow & Co., New York. See also the foreword to the American edition by the writer of this book.

5. Unpublished master's thesis, 1947. Reference is also made to this study in reference note 9 of chapter IV.

6. Henry. *Supra.*

7. One of the best is *Pastoral Psychology*, published in Manhasset, New York.

8. From the Charter of The George W. Henry Foundation.

CHAPTER VIII

1. The term *gay* has found acceptance in homosexual circles as a synonym for the sexually deviated. Many, perhaps most, practising homosexuals seem to prefer it to the word *homosexual*, which is regarded as an epithet. Certainly *gay* can be used much more easily than some of the less flattering terms that are vulgarly employed to identify those who exercise their sexual propensities for their own sex. One is told that the term has become almost respectable.

2. Wildeblood. *A Way of Life, supra.*

3. A. A. Gross. *What Price the Individual?* New York: The George W. Henry Foundation, 1961.

4. Hebrews x: 32. (R.S.V.)

5. The phrase is borrowed from Ludwig Lewisohn who, a long time ago, wrote a book with those words for its title. In this work he spoke of the condition of other dwellers in a world-within-a-world the less discerning have long mistreated.

6. Wildeblood. *A Way of Life. Supra.*

7. Psalm cxviii: 22.

CHAPTER IX

1. From *Hugh: Memoirs of a Brother.* New York: Longmans, Green & Co., 1916.

2. George W. Henry. "Psychogenic Factors in Overt Homosexuality," *American Journal of Psychiatry,* Oct., 1937.

3. George W. Corner. "Science and Sex Ethics," *Saturday Evening Post,* October 10, 1959.

4. There was a certain irony in requiring the Wolfenden Committee to report on female prostitution as well as the homosexual offenses. It can be said that the "fairy" is not unlike his feminine counterpart who plies her trade on the streets. Both have been deprived of their dignity. Before they can be restored to a sense of their importance in the scheme of things, they must regain their self respect. Without it one is devoid of dignity. Early in this century Bouck White, a Christian Socialist preacher, wrote a book entitled *The Call of the Carpenter.* In it he tried to paraphrase the Sermon on the Mount in language he considered suitable for the needs of his day. One sentence stands out strikingly: "The Kingdom of God is the kingdom of self respect." He that hath ears to hear . . .

5. Henry and Gross. *Social Factors . . . supra.*

6. *The Life of the Spirit. Supra.*

7. President of Hebrew Union College, Cincinnati, Ohio. From Murrow: *This I Believe.* New York: Simon & Schuster, 1952.

8. Henry and Gross: *Social Factors . . . supra.*

CHAPTER X

1. From "The Law and the Future", *Fortune,* November, 1955.

2. No less weighty an authority than the Chief Justice of the U.S. Supreme Court reminds us not to forget the Declaration's admonition that the ultimate seat of authority lies in the consent of the governed. This he does in his dissent in the *Perez* case. (Perez v. Brownell, 356 U. S. 44-1958.)

3. In the *Summa Theologica.* As quoted in Wu, *Fountain of Justice, supra.*

4. Henry. *All the Sexes, supra.*

5. Despite the sling and arrows of outrageous fortune, homosexuals seem little prone to taking their own lives. In the course of twenty five years The George W. Henry Foundation encountered only two suicides. Of threats to end it all we have had our fair share. But a little soothing syrup (or castor oil, as the case may be) works wonders.

6. E. G. Lee. *Mass Man and Religion.* New York: Harper, 1944.

7. Referring to the Labouchere Amendment to the Offenses Against the Person Act,

that the House of Commons passed in the 1880's. It is under this act that English homosexuals are generally prosecuted. This is the law that was used by the Public Prosecutor to send Oscar Wilde to prison.

8. David Bryn-Jones. *The Dilemma of the Idealist*. New York: Macmillan Co., 1950.

9. *Ibid*.

10. From the Charter of The George W. Henry Foundation.

11. Oliver Wendell Holmes. *Collected Legal Papers, supra*.

12. First Book of Esdras, iv: 41.

INDEX